Stopwatch

Teacher's Guide

3

Ivor Williams

Richmond

Richmond

58 St Aldates
Oxford
OX1 1ST
United Kingdom

Stopwatch Teacher's Guide Level 3

First Edition: February 2016
ISBN: 978-607-06-1248-0

© Text: Ivor Williams
© Richmond Publishing, S.A. de C.V. 2016
Av. Río Mixcoac No. 274, Col. Acacias,
Del. Benito Juárez, C.P. 03240, México, D.F.

Publisher: Justine Piekarowicz
Editorial Team: Suzanne Guerrero, Kimberly MacCurdy, Cara Norris
Art and Design Coordinators: Jaime Angeles, Karla Avila
Design: Jaime Angeles, Karla Avila
Layout: Erick López, Daniel Mejía, Perla Zapien
Pre-Press Coordinator: Daniel Santillán
Pre-Press Team: Susana Alcántara, Virginia Arroyo, Daniel Santillán
Cover Design: Karla Avila
Cover Photograph: © **Thinkstock:** saintho
(Group yacht at regatta)

All rights reserved. No part of this work may be reproduced, stored in a retrieval system or transmitted in any form or by any means without prior written permission from the Publisher.

Richmond publications may contain links to third party websites or apps. We have no control over the content of these websites or apps, which may change frequently, and we are not responsible for the content or the way it may be used with our materials. Teachers and students are advised to exercise discretion when accessing the links.

The Publisher has made every effort to trace the owner of copyright material; however, the Publisher will correct any involuntary omission at the earliest opportunity.

Printed in Brazil by Forma Certa

Lote: 800374

Contents

- 4 Scope and Sequence
- 6 Introduction to the Teacher's Guide
- 10 Unit 0 Can learning be fun?
- 15 Unit 1 Why do we need rules?
- 29 Unit 2 What's the best job?
- 43 Unit 3 Do we really need all this stuff?
- 57 Unit 4 How do you protect the planet?
- 71 Unit 5 What does it mean to be happy?
- 85 Unit 6 Where do bright ideas come from?
- 99 Unit 7 When is the right time?
- 113 Unit 8 How do you feel?
- 127 Verb List

Scope and Sequence

Unit	Vocabulary	Grammar	Skills
0 **Can learning be fun?**	**Review:** rooms in a house, furniture, classroom objects, food, clothes, free-time activities	Verb *be*; *There is / are*; *Can*; Imperatives	**Reading:** Identifying the main idea
1 **Why do we need rules?**	**School Supplies:** calculator, dictionary, gym uniform, recorder, ruler, sneakers **School Subjects:** art, chemistry, English, geography, history, literature, math, music, physical education, Spanish, technology	Present simple; Adverbs of frequency: *always, never, often, sometimes, usually*; Prepositions of time: *in, on, at*	**Listening:** Identifying key words **Writing:** Describing one's morning routine **Project:** Creating an infographic
2 **What's the best job?**	**Jobs:** engineer, firefighter, hairstylist, pilot, receptionist, transit operator **Workplaces:** airport, factory, fire station, hotel, salon, train station	Present continuous; Prepositions of place: *on, at, in*	**Reading:** Identifying and distinguishing facts from opinions **Writing:** Describing an imaginary job **Project:** Researching and writing about a dream job
3 **Do we really need all this stuff?**	**Clothes:** belt, blouse, coat, dress, hat, jeans, jewelry, pants, scarf, shorts, skirt, sneakers, socks, sweater, T-shirt	Comparative and superlative adjectives	**Reading:** Skimming and scanning **Listening:** Identifying specific information **Project:** Designing a bulletin board
4 **How do you protect the planet?**	**Food:** apple, bread, carrot, flour, lettuce, lime, milk, onion, orange, salami, strawberry, sugar, potato, tomato	Countable and uncountable nouns; Quantifiers: *a lot of, some, a little, a few, any*; *How much, How many*	**Writing:** Organizing ideas in paragraphs **Speaking:** Interviewing a classmate **Project:** Creating a short video to promote a green attitude

Unit	Vocabulary	Grammar	Skills
5 **What does it mean to be happy?**	**Pastimes:** camping, dancing, doing cannonballs, drawing, hanging out with friends, making models, playing board games, popping a wheelie, rollerblading	Verb *be: was, were*; *There was / were*	**Reading:** Describing a photo **Speaking:** Describing a photo **Project:** Designing and conducting a survey
6 **Where do bright ideas come from?**	**The Scientific Method:** analyze data, ask a question, do an experiment, do research, draw conclusions, write a hypothesis **Adjectives and Prepositions:** busy with, excited about, good at, interested in, nervous about, worried about	Past simple	**Listening:** Anticipating information **Writing:** Researching and writing a biography **Project:** Preparing for a trip to Mars
7 **When is the right time?**	**Weather:** cloud, cloudy, fog, foggy, rain, rainy, snow, snowy, storm, stormy, sun, sunny, wind, windy	Future simple: *will*; Future: *going to*	**Reading:** Previewing to predict content **Speaking:** Storytelling **Project:** Making a poster
8 **How do you feel?**	**Feelings:** anger, angry, embarrassment, embarrassed, excitement, excited, fear, frightened, happiness, happy, jealousy, jealous, sadness, sad, worry, worried	Questions; *What and Which*	**Writing:** Expressing opinions in a review essay **Speaking:** Discussing movie reviews **Project:** Making a brochure

The Concept

Stopwatch is a motivating, six-level secondary series built around the concept of visual literacy.

- *Stopwatch* constructs students' language skills from A0 to B1 of the Common European Framework of Reference (CEFR).
- A stopwatch symbolizes energy, speed, movement and competition and gives immediate feedback. The *Stopwatch* series offers dynamic, engaging activities and timed challenges that encourage students to focus and train for mastery.
- *Stopwatch* has a strong visual component to facilitate and deepen learning through authentic tasks, compelling images and the use of icons.
- The series was conceived for the international market, with a wide range of topics, incorporating cultures from around the world.
- The six-level framework of the series allows for different entry points to fit the needs of each school or group of students.
- The syllabus has been carefully structured. Each level recycles and expands on the language that was used in the previous books. This process of spiraled language development helps students internalize what they are learning.
- Each level of *Stopwatch* covers 90 – 120 hours of classroom instruction, plus an additional 20 hours of supplementary activities and materials in the Teacher's Guide and Teacher's Toolkit.

The Components

Stopwatch contains a mix of print and digital resources including:
- Student's Book & Workbook with Audio (print and Digital Book)
- Teacher's Guide (print and Digital Book)
- Teacher's Toolkit
- Stopwatch App (an actual stopwatch with fun vocabulary activities)

Student's Book & Workbook

Units are divided into distinct spreads, each with a clear focus:
- A **Big Question** establishes the central theme of the unit and promotes critical thinking, curiosity and interest in learning.
- **Vocabulary** is presented in thematic sets and with rich visual support to convey meaning.
- **Grammar** is introduced in context, enabling students to see the meaning, form and use of the structure.
- **Skills** (reading, listening, writing and speaking) are developed through engaging topics.
- **Culture** invites the learner to immerse oneself in the rich variety of cultures and peoples on our planet.
- **Review** activities provide consolidated practice for each of the grammar and vocabulary areas.
- In the **Project**, students apply the skills they learned in the unit to a creative task built around the Big Question.
- **Just for Fun** is a page with fun activities that teachers can assign to fast finishers.
- The **Workbook** pages offer extended practice with the vocabulary, structures and skills of the unit.
- **The Student's Audio** contains all the listening material in the units.

Teacher's Guide

Brief instructions or summaries provide a quick guide for each Student's Book activity, including **answer keys** and **audio scripts**.

A fun and engaging **warm-up** activity reviews previous knowledge and prepares students for what will be seen in each lesson.

A **wrap-up** task practices newly-learned material. Warm-ups and wrap-ups usually take the form of games.

Extension tasks promote use of language in communication and real-life situations.

Digital options provide alternatives to the projects using electronic media.

Specific questions, related to the Big Question of the unit, stimulate critical thinking.

Teaching tips help develop and enrich teachers' skills.

Teacher's Toolkit

The **Teacher's Toolkit** is a comprehensive resource that is available on the Richmond Learning Platform <https://richmondlp.com>.

- **Two optional placement tests** (beginner and intermediate) will help teachers assess their students' level of English on an individual and group basis and guide them in their choice of level and test packages.
- **Two different test packages** each contain unit tests, midterm and final exams, as well as rubrics for evaluating unit projects. There are two packages to choose from:
The *Standard* **test pack** for grammar and vocabulary as well as reading and listening.

The *Test Plus* **test pack** includes an additional communication component to assess speaking and writing. The *Test Plus* package is intended for students who are able to do all of the extension tasks in the Teacher's Guide.

- **Audio** is available in mp3 format.
- **Answer Keys** and audio transcripts for tests are included.
- **Grammar and Vocabulary Worksheets** are provided to ensure sufficient practice opportunities.
- **Reading Worksheets** (Time reading texts) are provided to offer students opportunities to develop reading skills.
- **Scorecard** forms to print or project to help students evaluate their progress are available.

Stopwatch App

The **stopwatch function** should be used for the timed activities in the Student's Book and Workbook.

Vocabulary flashcard games help students memorize words using fast-paced, fun review tasks.

The Big Question: Where are you from?

Meaningful Language in Context

- **Teacher's Guide**
  - Extension activities
  - Digital options for the project

- **Student's Book & Workbook**

- **Teacher's Toolkit**
  - Additional readings

Unit Opener

Visual prompts establish context and promote discussion

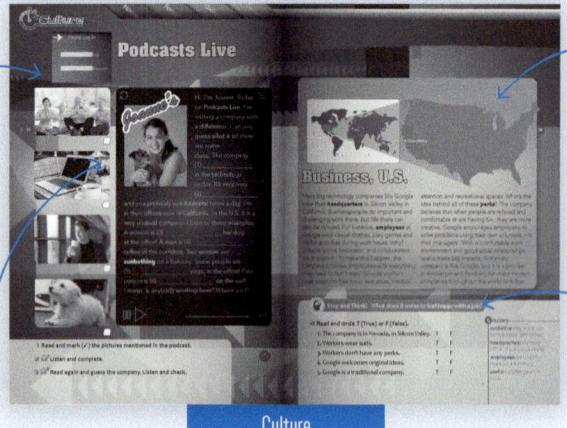

Skills

Two skills per unit

Tips for skills development

Skills development tasks

Glossary of new words

Critical Thinking tasks

Culture

Audio available on the platform and in the Digital Book

Content relevant to students' lives

Critical thinking / Value tasks

Level-appropriate language encourages learner engagement

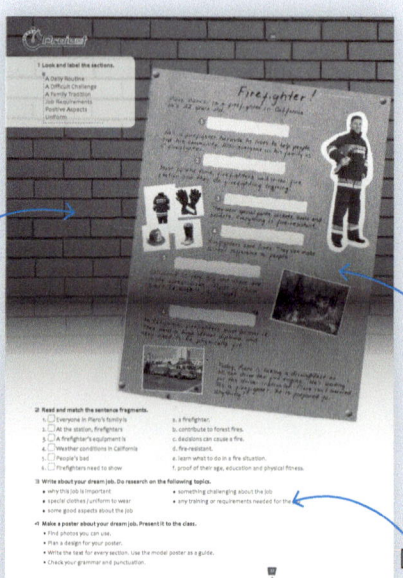

Project

Linguistic and conceptual preparation for the project

Vertical orientation of some sections to conform to visual requirements

Sample of project

Digital options for the project in Teacher's Guide

Strong Linguistic Focus

- **Teacher's Guide**
  - Warm-ups and wrap-ups
  - Teaching tips

- **Student's Book & Workbook**

- **Teacher's Toolkit**
  - Exams and exam audio
  - Vocabulary worksheets
  - Grammar worksheets

Visual literacy development

Vocabulary

imed, ame-like ctivity

Insight to language or content

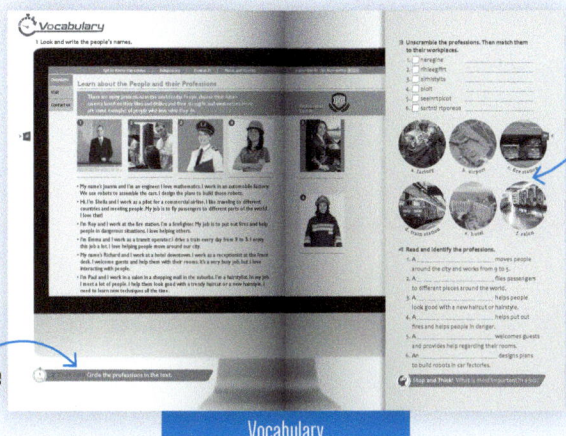

Grammar

Activities for fast finishers

Just for Fun

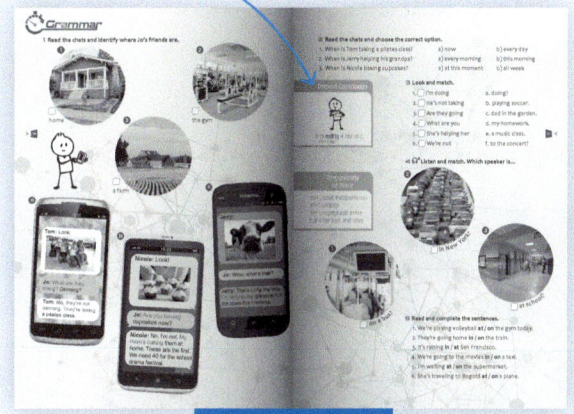

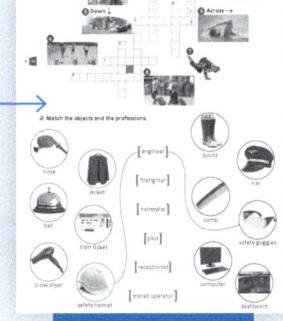

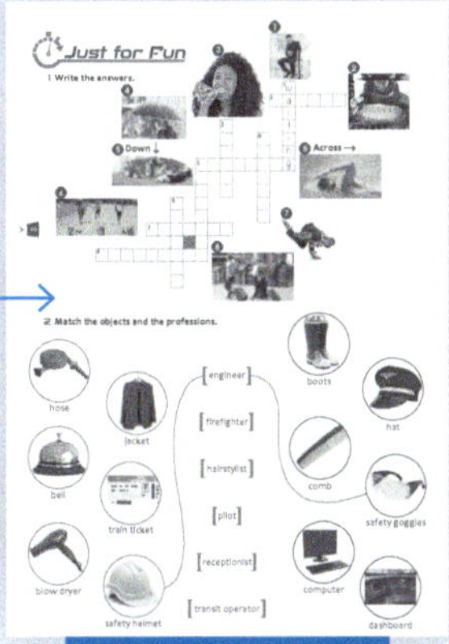

Topics expand on the unit theme

Review

More practice with unit grammar and vocabulary

Workbook section

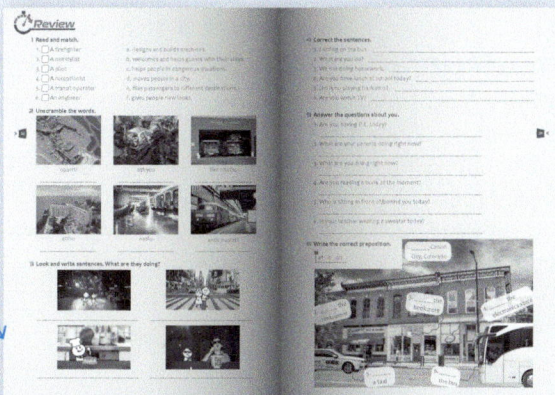

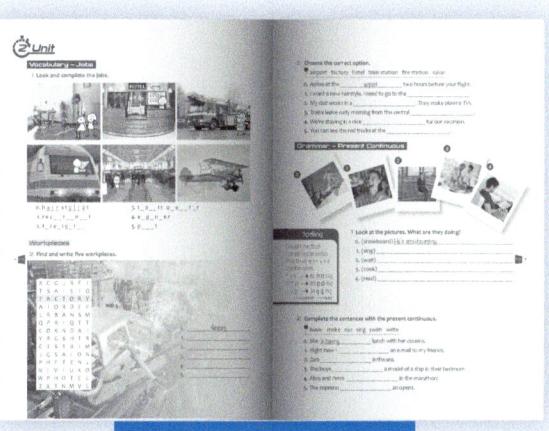

0 Can learning be fun?

Grammar	Vocabulary
Verb *be*: Are you good at Sudoku puzzles? Yes, I am. **There is/are**: There is a boy with a hat. **Can**: My teacher can speak Japanese. **Imperatives**: Practice every week. Don't go to bed late.	**Review**: rooms in a house, furniture, classroom objects, food, clothes, free-time activities

Reading
Identifying the main idea

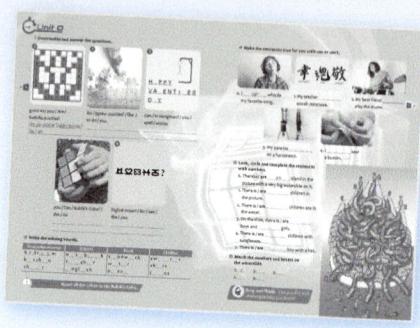

Teaching Tip
Teacher Expectations
Make clear what you expect from students at the beginning of a new course. You might want to mention some or all of the following:
- Students should make an effort to participate in class.
- Making mistakes is a natural part of the learning process, and students shouldn't be afraid or embarrassed if they say something incorrectly.
- Students should be prepared to work on their own outside class.
- Students should know that it's perfectly okay to ask for help if they need it.

Teaching Tip
Keeping a Vocabulary Notebook
Ask students to create a vocabulary notebook. They can make one using sheets in a binder or designate a few pages at the back of their notebooks. You can suggest they organize it by lexical sets. As they progress through the course, encourage students to add new words to the appropriate existing or new sections of their vocabulary notebooks.

Objective
Students will be able to identify **house**, **school**, **food** and **clothes** vocabulary.

Lesson 1   Student's Book p. 8

Warm-up
Students talk about the activities that they enjoy doing in English class.
- Ask students *What are some activities that you like doing in English class?* Students may mention games, puzzles, etc. Invite them to share comments.

1 Unscramble and answer the questions.
Students unscramble and answer questions about puzzle activities.

Answers
1. Do you like to do jigsaw puzzles? Yes, I do. / No, I don't. 2. Can you spell words in Hangman? Yes, I can. / No, I can't. 3. Can you do the Rubik's Cube? Yes, I can. / No, I can't. 4. Do you see the logical order? Yes, I do. / No, I don't.

2 Write the missing vowels.
Students review a selection of vocabulary items by writing the missing vowels.

Answers
House/Apartment kitchen, chair
School notebook, teacher, English
Food sandwich, water, pizza
Clothes sweater, skirt, jeans

3 Think Fast! Name all the colors in the Rubik's Cube.
Students do a one-minute timed challenge: they review colors vocabulary in a quiz question.

Answers
green, blue, yellow, orange, white, red

> ### Extension
> Students create their own crossword puzzles.
> - Tell students to look at the crossword puzzle on page 24 of their Student's Book and use it as a model.
> - Suggest that students use the vocabulary words in Activities 2 and 3 for their puzzles.
> - After they have made their puzzles, students can exchange them and complete each other's crosswords.

Wrap-up
Students add more words to the groups of words in Activity 2.
- Ask students to add at least three more words to each of the categories in Activity 2.
- Have students share their lists with the rest of the class.

Answers
Answers will vary; examples:
House/Apartment bathroom, living room, table
School desk, pencil, classroom
Food chicken, carrot, milk
Clothes coat, T-shirt, pants

➡ **(No homework today.)**

 **Unit 0**

Objectives
Students will be able to use *can* to talk about abilities and use *there is / there are* to describe a picture.

Lesson 2   Student's Book p. 9

Warm-up
Students talk about things that they can and can't do.
- Write a numbered series of sentences about talents and abilities on the board, e.g., *1. I can swim. 2. I can juggle with three balls. 3. I can play a musical instrument. 4. I can do magic tricks.* etc. and have students write down each number on a piece of paper. Have them write *Yes* or *No* next to each number depending on whether they can do the activity.
- Invite students to talk about what they can and can't do.

 12

4 Make the sentences true for you with *can* or *can't*.
Students complete sentences according to what they can and can't do.

Answers
Answers will vary.

5 Look, circle and complete the sentences with numbers.
Students review singular and plural forms of *be* and *there is / there are* as they complete sentences with *there is* or *there are* and numbers.

Answers
1. are 25, 2. are seven, 3. are nine, six, 4. are six, 5. is one

6 Match the numbers and letters on the waterslide.
Students solve a puzzle in an illustration.

Answers
1. C, 2. A, 3. E, 4. B, 5. D

Stop and Think! Critical Thinking
Can puzzles and challenges help you learn?
- Organize students into groups of three and have them brainstorm ways in which puzzles and mental challenges can help people to learn.
- Invite groups to share their ideas with the rest of the class.

Wrap-up
Students write descriptions of their classroom and their school.
- Ask students to write two paragraphs, one about what there is in their classroom and one about what there is in their school, using *there is / there are*.
- Before students begin writing, brainstorm as a class some vocabulary for things that are in classrooms and schools and write students' ideas on the board. (*Board, desks, chairs, chalk, marker, books, pens, pencils, windows, doors, hallways,* etc.)
- Have students form groups of three or four and tell them to share their desciptions and suggest corrections if necessary.

➡ **(No homework today.)**

Objectives

Students will be able to use the **verb be** in present and identify the correct **imperatives** to give advice.

Lesson 3   Student's Book p. 10

Warm-up

Students describe their bedrooms.

- Organize students into pairs. Have them take turns describing their bedrooms for their partners to draw, using *there is / are*.
- When they have finished, ask them to check their partners' drawings.

7 Complete the questions with *are*, *is* or *there*. Then answer.

Students complete and answer questions using the verb *be* and *there is / are*.

Answers

1. *are*, Answers will vary. 2. is, Answers will vary. 3. are there, Answers will vary. 4. are there, Answers will vary.

8 Look and complete the corresponding lines in the text balloons.

Students match text balloons with photos.

Answers

1st balloon left photo, *2nd balloon* right photo

9 How do you play sports? Mark (✓) the opinion you agree with.

Students comment on their attitudes toward competitive sports.

- Read aloud the statements in the text balloons in the previous activity.
- Have students mark the opinion they agree with.
- Organize students into small groups and invite them to discuss which of the two opinions they most identify with. Encourage them to explain why they chose one statement over the other.

Answers

Answers will vary.

10 Read and circle the correct options.

Students select the correct imperative forms in a reading activity.

Answers

1. Respect, 2. Don't get, 3. Eat, 4. Drink, 5. Don't go, 6. Keep

Extension

Students create posters giving advice.

- Brainstorm possible topics as a class, such as "Healthy Eating" or "Being a Good Athlete."
- Have students work in small groups to create posters giving advice about the topic of their choice using imperatives.
- Display students' posters around the classroom.

Wrap-up

Students play a game to practice using imperatives.

- Tell students to focus on the imperatives in bold in Activity 10 (and ignore the rest of each sentence).
- In small groups, have students sit in circles and go around the circle using each imperative form (both affirmative and negative) in a new sentence. Tell students to try to think of sentences as quickly as possible.
- The group who finishes making sentences with all twelve of the imperatives first wins.

 **(No homework today.)**

Teaching Tip
Managing Projects

When giving students any type of project work, make sure that students understand clearly what they have to produce and how long they have to produce it. A clear end product and a clear time frame will help to focus students' attention on the task and help them to avoid wasting time.

 Unit 0

Objective
Students will be able to identify the main idea of an article.

Lesson 4 Student's Book p. 11

Warm-up
Students discuss eyesight using *can* and *can't*.
- As a whole-class activity, discuss the kinds of activities that become difficult if we have problems with eyesight. Ask *If you can't see clearly, what things can you not do?*
- Elicit answers using *can't*: You can't drive. You can't read a book.
- Now ask *What can you do instead?* Elicit answers using *can*: You can wear glasses. You can learn braille.

11 Look at the pictures in the article. Can you see hidden messages?
Students look at images to find hidden information.
- Tell students to look at the images in the article and see if they can find any hidden messages in them.

12 Read the article and mark (✓) the main idea.
Students identify the main idea of a text.

Answer
2

13 Label the visual problems with the pictures.
Students match descriptions of medical conditions with photos.

Answers
1. c, 2. a, 3. b

14 🎧 Listen and check your answers.
Students listen to check information.

Audio Script
1. Boy: Grandpa, what happened?
   Grandpa: Oh, I can't see well when the cup isn't in my hand.
   Boy: Oh, you don't see well in 3-D.
   Grandpa: Of course I'm not a hero from a 3-D movie, young man. I'm just old!
2. Teacher: Owen, what's the answer?
   Boy: Umm… The French Revolution?
   Teacher: Owen, I think you need glasses.
   Girl: Or maybe you need to study, Owen!
3. Girl: Dad! Remember that your pink shirt is on the left in the closet, and the green one is on the right.
   Father: Oh, OK. I forgot.

Stop and Think! Critical Thinking
Are you ready to start this year of English classes?
- Organize students into small groups and have them draw up a list of New School Year Resolutions: things that they plan to do to get the new year off to a good start.
- Invite groups to share their ideas with the rest of the class.

❓ Big Question
Students are given the opportunity to revisit the Big Question and reflect on it.
- Ask students to turn to the unit opener on page 7 and look again at the photo, which shows a maze and a sign that reads CHALLENGES AHEAD.
- Ask students if they have ever been in a maze and invite them to share or imagine what it feels like to try to get to the center of a maze.
- Try to elicit the idea that it takes effort to find the center of a maze, but that it is also fun. From this idea, explain to students that in this level of the course they will face challenges, but that it will also be fun.
- Ask students *What makes learning fun for you?* Discuss as a class.

▶ **(No homework today.)**

1 Why do we need rules?

Grammar

Present simple: She studies at night.

Adverbs of frequency: *always, never, often, sometimes, usualy*: I usually eat there.

Prepositions of time: *in, on, at*: Pete has art in the afternoon. We don't go to school on the weekend.

Vocabulary

School Supplies: calculator, dictionary, gym uniform, recorder, ruler, sneakers

School Subjects: art, chemistry, English, geography, history, literature, math, music, physical education, Spanish, technology

Listening

Identifying key words

Writing

Describing one's morning routine

Why do we need rules?

In the first lesson, read the unit title aloud and have students look carefully at the unit cover. Encourage them to think about the message in the picture. At the end of the unit, students will discuss the big question: *Why do we need rules?*

Teaching Tip

Setting Ground Rules for Discussions

At the start of the course, establish some clear ground rules for group and whole-class discussions. Make clear the importance of taking turns to speak, of listening respectfully when someone else is speaking, of expressing disagreement in a way that is not offensive, etc.

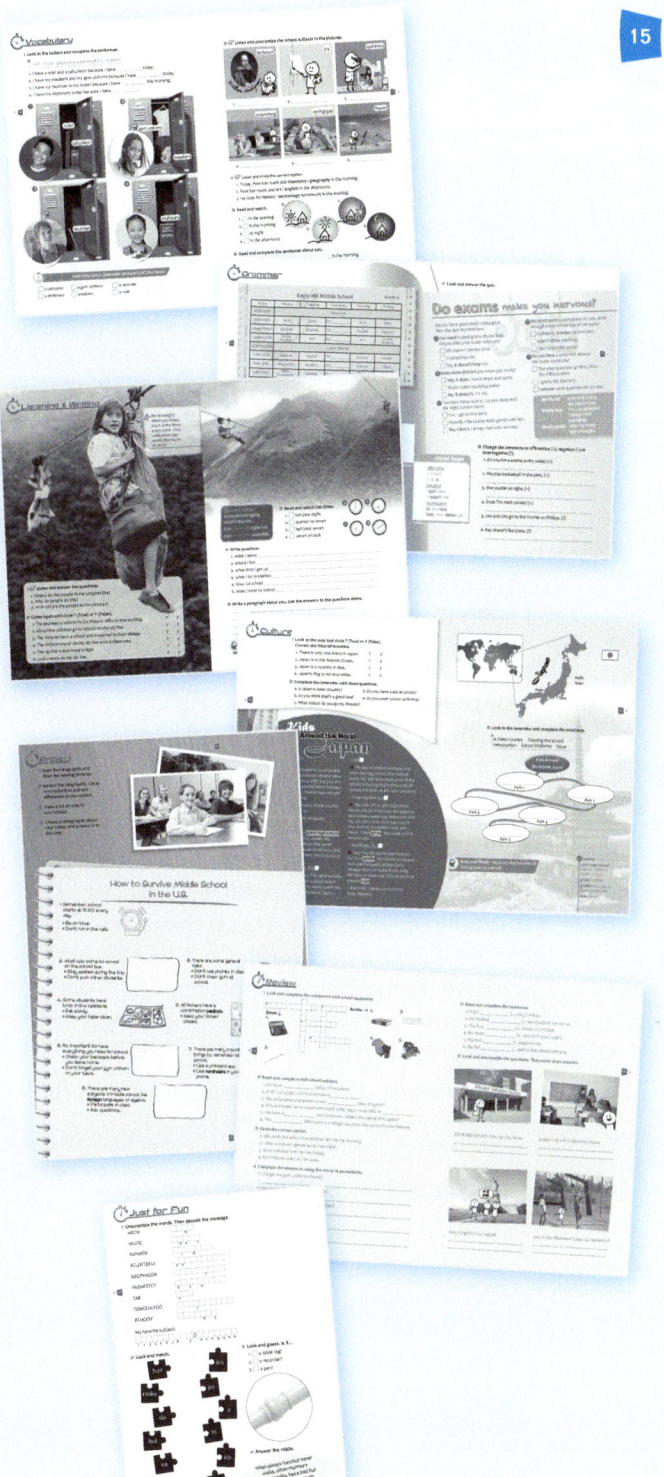

Vocabulary

> **Objective**
> Students will be able to use **school subjects** and **school objects** vocabulary to talk about their classes.

Lesson 1 Student's Book p. 14

Warm-up

Students select adjectives that they feel describe their school.
- Keeping in mind the Big Question on the previous page, write a variety of adjectives that could describe a school (*strict, friendly, noisy, neat, chaotic, orderly, relaxed*, etc.) on the board and invite students to say which ones best describe their own school.
- Encourage students to discuss their ideas as a whole class. Ask *Do the rules at our school affect what school is like? How?*

1 Look at the lockers and complete the sentences.
Students practice school subjects vocabulary while using it to complete sentences.

Answers
1. math, 2. physical education (P.E.), 3. music, 4. Spanish

2 Think Fast! Interview your classmate and mark (✓) the items.
Students do a three-minute timed challenge: they exchange information about the school equipment and items that they have with them.

Answers
Answers will vary.

Wrap-up

Students write about the equipment and the items that they have with them according to different days of the week.
- Tell students to write at least five sentences explaining the school items that they have with them on different days for the various subjects that they have on those days. For example, a student might write, *On Mondays, I have my gym uniform with me because I have P.E.*
- Invite students to share their sentences with the rest of the class.

➡ **Workbook p. 126, Activities 1 and 2**

Lesson 2   Student's Book p. 15

> ✔ **Homework Check!**
> Workbook p. 126, Activities 1 and 2
> **Answers**
> **1 Look and label the pictures.**
> 1. recorder, 2. gym uniform, 3. pencil, 4. sneakers, 5. eraser, 6. calculator, 7. ruler, 8. dictionary, 9. pen
> **2 Correct one mistake in each sentence.**
> 1. ~~literature~~ You need a calculator for your <u>math</u> class. 2. ~~pencil~~ This <u>dictionary</u> contains a lot of words. 3. ~~ruler~~ You can make very nice music with a <u>recorder</u>. 4. ~~art~~ Bring your gym uniform because we have <u>P.E.</u> today.

Warm-up
Students sort school objects into groups.
- Show students a selection of items (e.g., a globe, an atlas, a ruler, compasses, etc.) and ask them to group them by school subject.

3 🎧² **Listen and unscramble the school subjects in the pictures.**
Students practice more school subjects vocabulary in a listening and spelling activity.

Answers

1. literature, 2. art, 3. chemistry, 4. technology, 5. geography, 6. history

Audio Script
1. literature	l-i-t--e-r-a-t-u-r-e
2. art	a-r-t
3. chemistry	c-h-e-m-i-s-t-r-y
4. technology	t-e-c-h-n-o-l-o-g-y
5. geography	g-e-o-g-r-a-p-h-y
6. history	h-i-s-t-o-r-y

4 🎧³ **Listen and circle the correct option.**
Students choose the correct school subject to complete each sentence according to the audio.

Answers

1. chemistry, 2. English, 3. technology

Audio Script
Hi! I'm Pete. Today, I have math and …uh… chemistry in the morning. Then I have music and English in the afternoon. After school, I play basketball for the school team. I do my technology homework in the evening. I watch TV at night before I go to bed.

5 **Read and match.**
Students practice prepositions of time by matching phrases to the correct picture of each time of day.

Answers

1. a, 2. c, 3. d, 4. b

6 **Read and complete the sentences about you.**
In a personalization activity, students complete sentences with information about what they do at different times of day.

Answers

Answers will vary.

Wrap-up

Students discuss their favorite days of the week.
- Organize students into group of three or four.
- Have them talk about their favorite days of the week and explain why. Tell students to also mention what subjects they have and at what time on those days.

▶ **Workbook pp. 126 and 127, Activities 3 and 4**

 Grammar

Objectives
Students will be able to use **prepositions of time**, **adverbs of frequency** and the **present simple** to talk about school.

Lesson 3   Student's Book p. 16

> ✔ **Homework Check!**
> Workbook pp. 126 and 127, Activities 3 and 4
> **Answers**
> **3 Read and match.**
> 1. e, 2. b, 3. a, 4. c, 5. f
> **4 Read and complete the text.**
> 1. in, 2. in, 3. At

Warm-up

Students participate in a quick-fire quiz about their class schedule.
- Say a school day and a time, e.g., *Tuesday at ten o'clock* and ask students to say what subject they have.

1 🎧⁴ **Listen and complete the class schedule for Wednesday.**

Students complete a class schedule using school subjects vocabulary according to the audio.

Answers

1. Math, 2. English, 3. Band, 4. Science, 5. Geography, 6. P.E.

Audio Script

JIM: Britney! Do you know our schedule today?
BRITNEY: Yes, I do. Why?
JIM: Well, I don't have mine.
BRITNEY: Oh, OK. Well, we always have math at nine in the morning.
JIM: Yeah, I remember that! And we always have English at 10.
BRITNEY: Then for third period, we have...
JIM: Band! By the way, do we have any homework?
BRITNEY: No. We sometimes have band practice in the afternoon, but not this week. Then there's lunch. Do you eat at the school cafeteria?
JIM: Yeah, I usually eat there, but on Wednesdays, I bring my own lunch.
BRITNEY: Jim, where is your lunch?
JIM: In my backpack. Wait... Oh no! I don't have it! It's at home! Anyway, what classes do we have in the afternoon?

BRITNEY: We have science at one with Mr. Porter.
JIM: Cool! And then reading?
BRITNEY: No, we never have reading on Wednesday. It's only on Tuesday.
JIM: Do we have geography at 2?
BRITNEY: Yes, we do. Then at 3 we have P.E. It's soccer practice today. Remember we often play soccer in December. It's the state tournament. Do you have your soccer uniform today?
JIM: Oh yes, I do. It's right here in my locker.

2 🎧⁴ **Listen again and choose the correct option.**
Students are exposed to adverbs of frequency while they choose the correct options to complete the sentences according to the audio.

Answers

1. morning, 2. afternoon, 3. Wednesdays, 4. Tuesday, 5. December

3 Look and complete the chart.
Students complete a chart with adverbs of frequency.

Answers

from left to right never, sometimes, *often*, usually, always

Wrap-up

Students describe their routines.
- Tell students to write five true sentences about what they do and when, using adverbs of frequency and prepositions of time.
- Organize students into small groups and have them share their sentences.

➡ **Workbook p. 128, Activity 4**

Lesson 4 Student's Book p. 17

> ✔ **Homework Check!**
> Workbook p. 128, Activity 4
> **Answers**
> **4 Read and complete the sentences.**
> 1. sometimes, 2. usually, 3. always, 4. never

Warm-up
Students play an association game, using feelings.
- Brainstorm feelings with students and write them on the board.
- Tell students they are going to play an association game. You will say a word and they will write the how it makes them feel.
- Say the following words: *music, math, P.E., homework, lunch, weekends, exam*. As you say each word, write it on the board. Students will write how each word makes them feel.
- Form groups of three or four students and have them share how each word makes them feel.
- Ask students *How do exams make you feel?*

4 Look and answer the quiz.
Students are exposed to the interrogative, affirmative and negative forms of the present simple as they complete a quiz about exams and exam preparation.

Answers
Answers will vary.

5 Change the sentences to affirmative (+), negative (–) or interrogative (?).
Students practice writing sentences (affirmative, negative, or interrogative) in the present simple.
- Draw students' attention to the **Present Simple** box with information about the affirmative, negative and interrogative forms of the present simple.

Answers
1. I have exams every week. 2. We don't play basketball in the park. 3. She doesn't study at night. 4. Tim reads novels. 5. Do Joe and Lisa go to the movies on Fridays? 6. Does Ray like pizza?

Wrap-up
In small groups, students design and write quizzes similar to the one on this page. The quizzes can be about free-time activities, friends, daily routines, etc. and should include questions in the present simple. After they finish writing their quizzes, groups can exchange them and answer the questions.

 **Workbook pp. 127 and 128, Activities 1–3**

> **Teaching Tip**
> **Having Students Explain the Topic**
> Students show that they have understood a grammatical structure when they can explain it to others. Invite students to create posters illustrating the forms of the present simple. Display the posters around the classroom. Repeat this with other grammatical structures that students study later on.

Listening & Writing

Objectives
Students will be able to identify key information in a listening. They will also be able to describe their morning routines.

Lesson 5   Student's Book pp. 18 and 19

> ✔ **Homework Check!**
> Workbook pp. 127 and 128, Activities 1–3
> **Answers**
> **1 Look and circle the correct option.**
> 1. has, 2. studies, 3. drive, 4. goes, 5. speak, 6. does
> **2 Make negative sentences.**
> 1. I don't want a dog. 2. My mom doesn't drive the school bus. 3. Melanie doesn't have your ruler. 4. They don't speak Japanese. 5. You don't play soccer in the afternoon.
> **3 Read and complete the conversation with** *do* **or** *does***.**
> 1. do, 2. do, 3. don't, 4. Does, 5. doesn't, 6. Does, 7. does

Warm-up
Students talk about how they get to school.
- Write *bus, train, car, by foot, bike* on the board.
- Ask students how they get to school, how long it takes them, and how far they travel each day.

1 ⁵ **Listen and answer the questions.**
Students listen to an interview and identify key information needed to answer questions.

Answers

1. They live in the village of Los Pinos in Colombia., 2. Because they don't have a teacher in their village, and they don't have any other means of transportation., 3. They are about five to ten years old.

Audio Script
[P = Presenter, J = José, a Colombian teenager]
P: How do you get to school every day? Do you have a long journey on the bus? For the kids in the village of Los Pinos in Colombia, the journey to school is very difficult and dangerous. We talked to José, a Colombian boy, about his journey. José, how do the kids here get to school?
J: They use a zip line over the river. They don't have a bus. They don't have a train or a subway. They just have the zip line.
P: How many children do this?
J: About five children travel like this.
P: How old are they?
J: They're very young. They are about 5 to 10 years old.
P: Do they go on the zip line every day?
J: Yes, they do. They travel to school like this every day.
P: Why do they do this?
J: We live in the mountains. We have a school here in the village, but we don't have a teacher, so they travel to another school every day, on this zip line.
P: Do they travel on their own?
J: No, they don't. These children go to elementary school, so they travel with a parent or an adult.
P: Does the zip line go very high?
J: Yes, it does. It's 800 meters high!
P: That's amazing. Do you go on the zip line?
J: No, I don't. Not anymore, but I used to when I was in elementary school. Would you like to travel on the zip line?
P: Oh, no. Thank you, but no. Thank you for talking to us, José.
J: *De nada, señor*.

2 Listen again and circle T (True) or F (False).
Students listen for detailed information to determine whether statements about the interview are true or false.

Answers

1. T, 2. T, 3. F (The children don't have a teacher in their village.), 4. F (The children travel with a parent or an adult.), 5. T, 6. F (Jose doesn't travel on the zip line anymore.)

Wrap-up
Students role-play interviews with children from Los Pinos.

▶ **Workbook p. 129, Activity 1**

> 💭 **Teaching Tip**
> **Managing Fast Finishers**
> Some students complete activities more quickly than others, so it's a good idea to have a few extra activities on hand, otherwise these students may become bored and disruptive. One set of activities designed for fast finishers are the *Just for Fun* pages. Students can work on these individually and then check their answers in the back of the Student's Book. The *Just for Fun* activities for this unit are on page 26.

Lesson 6   Student's Book pp. 18 and 19

✔ **Homework Check!**
Workbook p. 129, Activity 1
Answers
1 Read and circle *T* (True) or *F* (False).
1. F (Johnny's village is in the mountains.),
2. F (Johnny walks to school.), 3. T, 4. F
(Johnny is always on time.), 5. T, 6. T

Warm-up
Students review telling the time.
- Review telling the time by asking students what classes they have at different times of the day. For example, ask, *What class do you have at ten o'clock on a Friday?* or *What class do you have at half past eleven on a Monday?*

3 Read and match the times.
Students match times written in words with clock faces.
- Draw students' attention to the **Guess What!** box. Read the information aloud and ask students which style of telling the time they have heard people use more often.

Answers
1. d, 2. c, 3. b, 4. a

4 Write questions.
Students write *Wh-* questions using cues.

Answers
1. What is your name? 2. Where do you live?
3. What time do you get up? 4. What do you have for breakfast? 5. How do you get to school?
6. What do you wear to school?

5 Write a paragraph about you. Use the answers to the questions above.
Students write a paragraph using their own answers to the questions from the previous activity.

Answers
Answers will vary.

Extension
Invite students to find out about school students of their age in other countries around the world. Have them prepare short presentations as if in the role of another student. For example, *My name is Luiz. I live in Sao Paulo…*

Stop and Think! Critical Thinking
What rules are important to obey when you travel to school?
- Organize students into groups of three and have them write a list of at least five rules that students should follow when traveling to and from school.
- Invite groups to share their ideas with the rest of the class.

Wrap-up
Students interview each other.
- Have students work in pairs and interview each other using the questions from Activity 4. Tell students not to look at their paragraphs from Activity 5 when they answer.

▶ **Workbook p. 129, Activities 2 and 3**

Preparing for the Next Lesson
Ask students to look around on the website for an introduction to school life in Japan: goo.gl/MuHCvB.

 Culture

Objectives
Students will be able to compare and contrast different cultures and develop awareness of cultural diversity.

Lesson 7   Student's Book pp. 20 and 21

> ✔ **Homework Check!**
> Workbook p. 129, Activities 2 and 3
> **Answers**
> **2 Look and write the times using the words.**
> 1. It's twenty past eight. 2. It's three o'clock.
> 3. It's half past twelve. 4. It's quarter past four.
> 5. It's five to seven.
> **3 Read the article again and rewrite it from Johnny's point of view.**
> Answers will vary.

Warm-up
Students answer general knowledge questions about Japan.
• Have students close their books. Conduct a quick-fire quiz about Japan. Ask, for example, *What continent is Japan in? What is the capital city of Japan? What money do they use in Japan? What is the population of Japan?*
Answers
Asia, Tokyo, yen, approximately 127 million

1 Look at the map and circle *T* (True) or *F* (False). Correct the false information.
Students use a map to determine whether statements are true or false and correct any false statements.
Answers
1. F (There are four major islands in Japan.), 2. F (Japan is in the Pacific Ocean.), 3. T, 4. T

2 Complete the interview with these questions.
Students read and complete an interview with the questions that correspond to each answer.
Answers
1. c, 2. e, 3. d, 4. b, 5. a

Wrap-up
Students discuss the content of the text.
• As a whole class, discuss ways in which Masako's school is similar to or different from the students' school. Encourage students to compare and contrast and express their ideas without being judgmental.

 (No homework today.)

Lesson 8   Student's Book pp. 20 and 21

Warm-up
Students review what they have learned about Japan so far.
- With their books closed, give small groups one minute to talk about what that they can remember about Japan.
- As a whole class, share answers.

3 Look at the interview and complete the mind map.
Students complete a visual summary of a text.

Answers
Part 1 Introduction, *Part 2* School Uniforms, *Part 3* Cleaning the School, *Part 4* Value, *Part 5* A Clean Country

Stop and Think! Critical Thinking
What are the benefits of having rules at school?
- Organize students into small groups and have them draw up a list of the benefits of having rules in a school.
- Conduct a whole-class discussion in which students share their ideas.
- Write on the board the ideas that the majority of students agree with.

Wrap-up
Students discuss ideas for a new rule.
- As a whole class, discuss students' ideas for a new rule for their school, that is, a rule that they believe is necessary and beneficial, but that is not part of the existing school rules.

 **(No homework today.)**

> 🐝 **Teaching Tip**
> **Using Mind Maps**
> Mind maps can be used in various ways, not just for creating a summary of a reading or listening text. Show students how to use mind maps as a way of sorting vocabulary, for example, or as a way of brainstorming ideas for a piece of writing.

Project

Objective
Students will be able to create an infographic.

Lesson 9 — Student's Book pp. 22 and 23

Warm-up
Students discuss the concept of an infographic.
- Write the word *infographic* on the board and ask students to separate it into its two parts (*info* and *graphic*).
- Discuss the meanings of these two parts of the word. Elicit or explain that *info* is an abbreviation for *information* and that *graphic* relates to visual art, especially drawing or writing. Thus an infographic is a visual representation of information or data. Discuss how infographics are intended to present information quickly and clearly.

1 Read the infographic and draw the missing pictures.
Students complete an infographic with simple illustrations.

Answers
Answers will vary.

2 Review the infographic. Circle two similarities and two differences in your school.
Students find similarities and differences between the school rules presented in an infographic and their own school.

Answers
Answers will vary.

Wrap-up
Students compare visual ideas and vote for their favorites.
- Invite students to submit their individual proposals for an image to go with, for example, Rule 2 on the infographic. Have the class vote for their favorite images for each rule.

Lesson 10   Student's Book pp. 22 and 23

Warm-up
Students brainstorm places that need to have sets of rules.
- As a whole class, brainstorm ideas about places and organizations that need rules in order to ensure that people are safe and that things run smoothly, e.g., places of work such as factories and offices, public spaces such as shopping malls, football stadiums, etc.

3 Make a list of rules in your school.
In small groups, have students write a list of rules for their school in preparation for creating an infographic.

4 Create an infographic about your school and present it to the class.
Students create an infographic showing the rules at their school.
- Ask students to work in the same small groups as in Activity 3. Encourage them to consider the layout and design of their infographics and the connections between textual and visual elements.
- Invite students to present their finished infographics to the rest of the class.

Extension
- Once students have shared their infographics with their own class, invite them to present their work to other classes or to members of staff.
- A selection of infographics could be displayed in an exhibition of students' work.

The Digital Touch
To incorporate digital media in the project, suggest one or more of the following:
- Have students present their infographics using PowerPoint or similar slide show presentation programs like Google Slides.
- Invite students to create videos using live actors, animation, voiceovers combined with images, etc.
- Encourage students to use free downloadable poster-making programs for their infographics.
- If possible, allow students to upload their work to the school's website.

Note that students should have the option to do a task on paper or digitally.

Wrap-up
Students compare infographics and vote for their favorites.
- Invite students to vote for their favorite infographics. There can be awards in various categories, e.g., best layout and design, best use of technology, best overall infographic, etc.

➤ **Workbook p. 128, Activity 1 (Review)**

 Teaching Tip
Managing Group Work
Teenagers usually enjoy working in teams. To ensure that group work goes well, conduct an oral evaluation after a task such as this project in which you ask students to reflect on how much they participated in their group, how they shared tasks, how well they cooperated, how much they listened to the other people in their team, how they came to decisions, how they resolved differences of opinion, etc.

Review

Objective
Students will be able to consolidate their understanding of the vocabulary and grammar learned in the unit.

Lesson 11 — Student's Book p. 24

> ✔ **Homework Check!**
> Workbook p. 128, Activity 1
> **Answers**
> **1 Complete about you!**
> Answers will vary.

 26 **Warm-up**
Students discuss their favorite school subjects.
- As a whole-class activity, invite students to say what their favorite subjects are and why and to talk a little about those subjects. Encourage them to use vocabulary and expressions that have been covered in this unit, e.g., school objects, times of day, etc.

1 Look and complete the crossword with school equipment.
Students complete a crossword using school objects vocabulary.

Answers
Down 1. calculator, 3. recorder
Across 2. dictionary, 3. ruler, 4. uniform, 5. sneakers

2 Read and complete with school subjects.
Students complete the sentences with the school subjects that make sense in each.

Answers
1. physical education (P.E.), 2. math, 3. technology, 4. history, 5. geography, 6. chemistry

3 Circle the correct option.
Students select the correct prepositions of time to complete each sentence.

Answers
1. in, 2. at, 3. on, 4. in

4 Complete the sentences using the words in parentheses.
Students practice word order with frequency adverbs by writing complete sentences.

Answers
1. I never forget my gym uniform. 2. We sometimes eat lunch at school. 3. Our teacher often gives us homework. 4. I usually watch TV after school. 5. Does Kim always sit next to you?

Wrap-up
Students write their own sentences using frequency adverbs.
- Challenge students to write five sentences that use a frequency adverb, a school subject and a piece of school equipment, for example, *On Mondays, I always take my calculator because we have math.*

➠ **(No homework today.)**

Lesson 12   Student's Book p. 25

Warm-up
Students play Hangman to review school subjects and school objects vocabulary.
- Invite students to play Hangman in teams. They should use vocabulary related to school subjects and school equipment.

5 Read and complete the sentences.
Students complete affirmative and negative sentences in the present simple.

Answers
1. plays, 2. doesn't have, 3. leaves, 4. watches, 5. doesn't play, 6. doesn't eat

6 Look and unscramble the questions. Then write short answers.
Students unscramble questions in the present simple and write answers to them according to the pictures.

Answers
1. Does she go to JFK Middle School? No, she doesn't. 2. Do we have chemistry today? Yes, we do. 3. Do they speak English? No, they don't. 4. Do you play basketball in the afternoon? Yes, I do.

 Big Question

Students are given the opportunity to revisit the Big Question and reflect on it.
- Ask students to turn to the unit opener on page 13 and look again at the picture, which shows signs prohibiting certain actions.
- Select one of the signs, for example, the one prohibiting the use of bicycles and discuss with students the places where this is a good rule (inside a school) and the places where it is not necessary (a public park). Repeat with some of the other signs.
- Organize students into small groups and have them try to complete the following sentence in just 50 words: *We need rules because…*

 Scorecard
Hand out (and/or project) a *Scorecard*. Have students fill in their *Scorecards* for this unit.

Study for the unit test.

Teaching Tip
Creating Exercises for Further Practice
At the end of this review section, and at the end of subsequent reviews, invite students to try writing their own practice exercises based on the material on these pages. The exercises can be for practicing vocabulary or grammar. Students can make copies of their exercises and exchange them with their classmates.

2 What's the best job?

Grammar	Vocabulary
Present continuous: They <u>are dancing</u>. I <u>am not taking</u> the train. **Prepositions of place:** *on, at, in*: We are <u>on</u> a bus <u>in</u> New York City.	**Jobs:** engineer, firefighter, hairstylist, pilot, receptionist, transit operator **Workplaces:** airport, factory, fire station, hotel, salon, train station

Reading	Writing
Identifying and distinguishing facts from opinions	Describing an imaginary job

What's the best job?

In the first lesson, read the unit title aloud and have students look carefully at the unit cover. Encourage them to think about the message in the picture. At the end of the unit, students will discuss the big question: *What's the best job?*

Teaching Tip
Guiding Peer Correction

Students often help each other by providing answers when their classmates are unsure and slow to respond. You can take advantage of this tendency and make error correction a collaborative learning experience. If time allows for it, you can have students exchange notebooks and check each other's work. Another opportunity for peer correction is when students are giving presentations in small groups. By encouraging peer correction, students become more aware not only of their classmates' language, but also of their own.

 Vocabulary

Objective
Students will be able to use **professions** and **workplaces** vocabulary to talk about what people do.

Lesson 1   Student's Book pp. 28 and 29

Warm-up

Students vote for the job(s) that they find the most appealing.
- Tell students to turn to page 27 and look at the photos of people doing a variety of jobs. Ask them to vote for the most appealing job. In a whole-class discussion, encourage students to say why they voted for one job over the others.

1 Look and write the people's names.
Students identify people's professions by matching the names given in descriptions with photos.

Answers
1. Richard, 2. Paul, 3. Sheila, 4. Joanna, 5. Emma, 6. Roy

2 Think Fast! Circle the professions in the text.
Students do a one-minute timed challenge: they scan the text to identify professions vocabulary.

Answers
engineer, pilot, firefighter, transit operator, receptionist, hairstylist

> **Extension**
> - Elicit or point out that the photos on these pages show a few instances of professions that, until relatively recently, very few women practiced or that were not even available to women.
> - Discuss how nowadays there are women who are pilots with commercial airlines, engineers, politicians, astronauts, CEOs of major companies, etc.

Wrap-up

Students practice professions vocabulary in the context of people they know.
- Form small groups and have students share information about family members, friends, and neighbors who work in the professions featured on these pages. Encourage them to describe what people do in their jobs.
- Invite each group to briefly summarize what their family and friends do.

➡ **Workbook p. 130, Activity 1**

Lesson 2   Student's Book p. 29

> ✔ **Homework Check!**
> Workbook p. 130, Activity 1
> **Answers**
> **1 Look and complete the jobs.**
> 1. receptionist, 2. firefighter, 3. transit operator,
> 4. engineer, 5. pilot

Warm-up
Students review professions vocabulary.
- Read aloud a sentence from the text on the previous page, for example, *I drive a train every day from 9 to 5.* and have students try to name the corresponding profession (transit operator).

3 Unscramble the professions. Then match them to their workplaces.
Students identify professions vocabulary and match professions with the corresponding workplaces.

Answers

1. engineer, a, 2. firefighter, c, 3. hairstylist, f,
4. pilot, b, 5. receptionist, e, 6. transit operator, d

4 Read and identify the professions.
Students complete sentences describing people's jobs with the correct professions.

Answers

1. transit operator, 2. pilot, 3. hairstylist,
4. firefighter, 5. receptionist, 6. engineer

Stop and Think! Critical Thinking
What is most important in a job?
- Organize students into small groups and have them brainstorm ideas about the various things that people value in a job, for example, working hours, interest and variety, pay, colleagues, job satisfaction, paid vacations, etc. (If necessary, write some ideas on the board to get them started.)
- Invite groups to share their ideas with the rest of the class.

Wrap-up
Students talk about their favorite jobs.
- Review the professions featured on these pages and the descriptions that tell what people do in each job.
- In small groups, have students talk about the jobs that they would most like to do.
- Invite individual students to share their reasons for voting for a particular job.

▶ **Workbook pp. 130 and 131, Activities 2 and 3**

# Grammar

Objective
Students will be able to use **present continuous** and **prepositions of place** to talk about what people are doing and where they are doing it.

Lesson 3   Student's Book pp. 30 and 31

✔ **Homework Check!**
Workbook pp. 130 and 131, Activities 2 and 3
Answers
2 Find and write five workplaces.

X	C	G	J	R	F	I
T	S	A	I	E	I	O
F	A	C	T	O	R	Y
A	I	O	R	D	E	E
L	R	B	A	N	S	M
Q	P	R	I	Q	T	T
C	O	K	N	D	A	I
Y	R	G	S	H	T	R
C	T	S	T	B	I	M
J	G	S	A	L	O	N
P	H	F	T	E	N	J
N	I	V	I	U	K	O
W	P	H	O	T	E	L
Z	X	T	N	M	V	L

airport, train station, fire station, salon, hotel
3 Choose the correct option.
1. salon, 2. factory, 3. train station, 4. hotel, 5. fire station

Warm-up
Students look at the photos to preview the lesson.
- Ask students *What do you see on the cell phones?* Elicit *photos and text messages.*
- Before students read the messages, ask *Do you ever send people photos using your cell phone? Why? Why do you think people sent each other those photos?* Have students discuss as a class.

1 Read the chats and identify where Jo's friends are.
Students are exposed to present continuous as they match the text messages to the correct places.
Answers
1. b, 2. a, 3. c

2 Read the chats and choose the correct option.
Students read the texts and identify when each person is doing the activity mentioned in the text.
- Draw students' attention to the *Present Continuous* box and read the information aloud. Remind students that the present simple is used for talking about routines, repeated actions and general truths, while the present continuous is used for actions that are happening at the moment.

Answers
1. a, 2. b, 3. a

Wrap-up
Students guess actions using the present continuous.
- Tell students to write five sentences using the present continuous. Have students include at least one sentence with each of the following pronouns: *I, you, he / she / it, they.*
- Tell students to form small groups. One person in each group mimes an action while the others guess what it is. Encourage students to use complete sentences, e.g., *You are playing soccer.*

 **Workbook p. 131, Activity 1**

💭 **Teaching Tip**
Using Metalanguage
Some students may recognize metalanguage such as *present simple* and *present continuous*, whereas others may be confused by it. Use grammatical terms and other metalanguage sparingly unless you're certain all students are familiar with them.

Lesson 4 Student's Book pp. 30 and 31

✔ **Homework Check!**

Workbook p. 131, Activity 1

Answers

1 Look at the pictures. What are they doing?
1. He is singing. 2. She is waiting. 3. They are cooking. 4. He is reading.

Warm-up

Students review the form of the present continuous with a simple dictation activity.

- Read aloud a series of verbs in their base form and ask students to simply write the *-ing* form of each verb. Be sure to include verbs that test students' memory of spelling rules, for example, *take-taking, swim-swimming, study-studying*.

3 Look and match.

Students practice common collocations related to everyday and free-time activities by matching the beginnings of the present continuous sentences with their correct endings.

Answers

1. d, 2. e, 3. f, 4. a, 5. c, 6. b

4 🎧⁶ Listen and match. Which speaker is...

Students are exposed to prepositions of place as they match each speaker to the photo of where the person is according to the audio.

Answers

1. 3, 2. 2, 3. 1

Audio Script

1. BRIAN: Hi, it's me, Brian. Today is a big day. I get to see my mom at work. She runs this place. I'm in her office now. Oh, gotta go. Classes are about to start.
2. COLIN: This is Colin. The city is huge! I'm here with my dad to see him at work. He's a salesperson for an important software company. The traffic here is impressive. Let me take a pic for you.
3. TINA: Hi. You're probably wondering where I am. I'm with my dad at his job. I have a chance to see a lot of nice places where we live. It's eight and there are a lot of people waiting to get to work.

5 Read and complete the sentences.

Students choose the correct prepositions of place to complete the sentences.

- Draw students' attention to the **Prepositions of Place** box and read the information aloud.

Answers

1. at, 2. on, 3. in, 4. in, 5. at, 6. on

Wrap-up

Students write sentences combining professions, prepositions of place and present continuous.

- Elicit a sentence with a preposition of place that tells us where somebody is now, for example, *Jenny is on a bus*. Then ask for another sentence that tells us what that person is doing, for example, *She is going to school*.
- Ask students to write five similar sentences, following this model. Invite students to share their sentences with the rest of the class.

➡ **Workbook p. 131, Activity 2**

Reading & Writing

Objectives
Students will be able to identify and distinguish facts from opinions. They will also be able to describe an imaginary job.

Lesson 5   Student's Book pp. 32 and 33

> ✔ **Homework Check!**
> Workbook p. 131, Activity 2
> **Answers**
> **2 Complete the sentences with the present continuous.**
> 1. am writing, 2. is swimming, 3. are making, 4. are running, 5. is singing

Warm-up
Students talk about unusual foods that they have tried.
- As a whole-class discussion, invite students to share stories of any unusual foods that they have tried and whether or not they enjoyed the experience.

1 Look at the pictures and the title of the article. What do you think it is about?
Students predict the content of an article from its title, pictures and layout.

2 Read the article and circle T (True) or F (False).
Students read the article and determine whether statements about the text are true or false.

Answers
1. F (She does the challenges before the TV show.), 2. T, 3. F (Sharon refuses to eat live animals because it's cruel.), 4. T

3 Find two facts and two opinions in the article. Write them in your notebook.
Students identify facts and opinions in the text.
- Draw students' attention to the *Be Strategic!* box and ask them to read the information. Make sure that students understand the difference between facts and opinions.

Answers
Answers will vary.

Wrap-up
Students exchange opinions about the information in a text.
- Ask students to look through the article and then elicit their opinions. Ask questions to elicit responses. Clarify that opinions are just that—people's views or judgments about something—and not necessarily based on facts or knowledge.

➡ **Workbook pp. 132 and 133, Activities 1 and 2 (Reading)**

 Teaching Tip
Managing Fast Finishers
Some students complete activities more quickly than others, so it's a good idea to have a few extra activities on hand, otherwise these students may become bored and disruptive. One set of activities designed for fast finishers are the *Just for Fun* pages. Students can work on these individually and then check their answers in the back of the Student's Book. The *Just for Fun* activities for this unit are on page 40.

Lesson 6
Student's Book pp. 32 and 33

✔ **Homework Check!**
Workbook pp. 132 and 133, Activities 1 and 2
Answers
1 Look at the title of the article. Guess the topic.
2. science
2 Read the article and circle *T* (True) or *F* (False).
1. F (Dr. Friend works on a boat.), 2. F (They are in the Indian Ocean.), 3. T, 4. T, 5. F (She often spends days on the boat and doesn't see anything.), 6. F (She prefers to see whales.)

Warm-up
Students read statements and distinguish between facts and opinions.
- Write on the board a series of statements, some facts and some opinions. Write, for example, *Many people watch celebrity survival reality shows.* (fact) and, *I think reality shows are a waste of time.* (opinion)
- Have students read the sentences and say which ones are facts and which ones are opinions.

4 Read the e-mail and number the sections.
Students read and identify the parts of an e-mail.
Answers
From top to bottom 2, 3, 1

5 Write an e-mail about an imaginary job you have.
Students think of an imaginary job and write an e-mail about what they do in the job, what they like and don't like about it and what they are currently doing at work.

Stop and Think! Critical Thinking
Can a job be dangerous? Is it OK?
- Organize students into small groups and have them draw up a list of jobs that involve some type of danger.
- Conduct a whole-class discussion about the dangerous jobs that students would or would not like to do, and why.
- Ask *Is it necessary that people do dangerous jobs? Why or why not? Is it OK that some people do more dangerous jobs than others?*

Wrap-up
Students share their e-mails about imaginary jobs.
- Students form pairs and share the e-mails they wrote in Activity 5.
- After reading each other's e-mails, students take turns interviewing each other about their imaginary jobs.
- Encourage students to ask each other about what they are doing at the moment, using present continuous.

➡ **Workbook p. 133, Activities 1 and 2**

Preparing for the Next Lesson
Ask students to view an introduction to what it is like to work at Google: goo.gl/MAq91b.

 **Culture**

Objectives
Students will be able to consider different approaches to work and places of work. They will also build awareness of the value of innovation.

Lesson 7   Student's Book pp. 34 and 35

> ✔ **Homework Check!**
> Workbook p. 133, Activities 1 and 2
> **Answers**
> **1 Circle 10 spelling mistakes. Then correct them.**
> 1. ~~too~~ to, 2. ~~whit~~ with, 3. ~~beautyful~~ beautiful, 4. ~~tyme~~ time, 5. ~~imporant~~ important 6. ~~meny~~ many, 7. ~~hom~~ home, 8. ~~momen~~ moment, 9. ~~grate~~ great, 10. ~~you~~ your
> **2 Choose a job and write an e-mail to Janet in your notebook.**
> Answers will vary.

Warm-up
Students discuss conventional office customs and practices.
- Elicit some of the things that people traditionally do in offices (*sit behind desks, use computers, talk on the phone, attend meetings, dress formally,* etc.).
- Also, try to elicit some of the things that people are traditionally not permitted or expected to do at work, for example, take their pets to work.

1 Read and mark (✓) the pictures mentioned in the podcast.
Students read a text and identify photos corresponding to things mentioned in the text.
Answers
1st, 3rd and 4th photos

2 🎧⁷ Listen and complete.
Students listen to part of a podcast and complete a transcription of it.
Answers
1. works, 2. famous, 3. keeping, 4. drinking, 5. doing, 6. writing

Audio Script
Hi, I'm Joanne. Today on *Podcasts Live*, I'm visiting a company with a difference. Can you guess what it is? Here are some clues.
The company works in the technology sector. It's very, very famous and you probably use it several times a day. I'm in their offices now in California, in the U.S. It is a very unusual company. Listen to these examples:
A woman is keeping her dog at the office!
A man is drinking coffee in the corridors.
Two women are sunbathing on a balcony.
Some people are doing yoga, in the office!
One person is writing on the wall!
I mean, is anybody working here?
Where am I?

3 🎧⁸ Read again and guess the company. Listen and check.
Students guess the identity of the company described in the podcast.
Answer
Google

Audio Script
Well, the answer is Google. Did you guess right? If you don't know an answer, you can google it! I'm at Google's headquarters in Mountain View, California, and by the way, did you know that...

> **Extension**
> Tell students to find out about other famous Internet companies that came into existence in recent years, for example, Yahoo!, Wikipedia, Facebook, etc.

Wrap-up
Students discuss working at Google.
- Elicit a summary of the podcast from the class. Ask *What do you think it would be like to work at Google?*
- Then tell students to raise their hands if they would like to work at Google. Ask *What do you like about it? Why would you want to work there?*
- Then ask students who did not raise their hands *What might not be good about working at Google? Why would you not want to work there?*

⏭ **(No homework today.)**

> 💭 **Teaching Tip**
> **Eliciting Responses**
> Eliciting responses invites students to become active participants in a class. Beginning students can often be hesitant to participate, so when you elicit information, avoid calling on any one student. If students don't immediately respond, be ready to provide a few examples to get a conversation or activity started.

Lesson 8
Student's Book p. 35

Warm-up
Students discuss technology companies.
- With books closed, ask students if they have heard of Silicon Valley. Elicit or explain that this term is a nickname for the southern part of the San Francisco Bay Area, in northern California and that it is home to many of the world's largest high-tech corporations.
- Then ask students if there is a region in their country where high-tech companies are concentrated. Invite students to share what they know.

4 Read and circle *T* (True) or *F* (False).
Students read the article and look for specific information. Then they determine whether statements about the text are true or false.

Answers
1. F (Silicon Valley is in California.), 2. F (Employees wear casual clothes.), 3. F (Workers have access to free food, rest areas, medical attention and recreational spaces.), 4. T, 5. F (Google is a pioneer in innovation and flexibility.)

Stop and Think! Critical Thinking
What does it mean to feel happy with a job?
- Organize students into small groups and have them brainstorm ideas about the things that make people happy in their places of work (pleasant surroundings, friendly co-workers, meaningful work, etc.)
- Invite groups to share their ideas with the rest of the class.

Wrap-up
Students role-play a conversation with an employee of a company like Google.
- Ask students to imagine themselves working for an innovative technology company such as Google.
- Organize students into pairs and have them work on a role play in which one student interviews an employee of a tech company and asks about the workplace and a typical day.

(No homework today.)

> ### Teaching Tip
> **Identifying Word Families**
> Encourage students to record and learn vocabulary items in word families. Taking an example from the text on this page, students can record *employee* and also *employer, employ, employment*, etc.

Project

Objective
Students will be able to research and write about a dream job.

Lesson 9
Student's Book pp. 36 and 37

Warm-up

Students categorize jobs according to different criteria.
- Elicit jobs students have seen in this unit and a few others that they are familiar with. Write a list on the board.
- Organize students into small groups and ask them to categorize the jobs in different ways. For example, they can make a group of dangerous jobs, of well-paid jobs, of jobs that people do outside, of technology jobs, etc.

1 Look and label the sections.

Students read and label the sections of a poster with the correct sub-headings.

Answers

1. A Family Tradition, 2. A Daily Routine,
3. Uniform, 4. Positive Aspects,
5. A Difficult Challenge, 6. Job Requirements

2 Read and match the sentence fragments.

Students match phrases to make complete sentences.

Answers

1. a, 2. e, 3. d, 4. b, 5. c, 6. f

Wrap-up

Students debate whether being a firefighter is a dream job.
- Divide the class into two teams. Ask *Is being a firefighter a dream job?* Assign the first team to argue that being a firefighter is a dream job and the other team to argue that it is not.
- Give teams a few minutes to brainstorm and note the reasons for their positions before beginning the debate.

Teaching Tip

Managing a Class Debate
In order to have a successful debate, students need to understand the stages of a debate and be aware of the time allotted for each stage. Explain the stages of a debate to your students. Then as you conduct the debate, set time limits for each stage: preparing opening statements, presenting supporting statements, preparing rebuttal, presenting rebuttal, etc.

Lesson 10   Student's Book pp. 36 and 37

Warm-up
Students share information about the workplaces of people they know.
- As a whole-class activity, elicit information, anecdotes, etc. about any time when they were able to visit the place of work of a person they know (a parent, a relative, a neighbor, etc.) or visit a place such as a fire station, a local factory, a police station, etc.

3 Write about your dream job. Do research on the following topics.

Students carry out research for their dream job posters.
- Read the five topics aloud and make sure that students understand the key ideas in words and phrases like *good aspects*, *challenging*, *requirements*.
- Tell students to research the topics, using books, magazines and other materials from the school library or a local library or by searching on the Internet.
- Have students take notes and summarize all the information that they find into sections as in the firefighter example on the page.

4 Make a poster about your dream job. Present it to the class.

Students design and create their dream job posters and present them to the class.

> **The Digital Touch**
>
> To incorporate digital media in the project, suggest one or more of the following:
> - Have students present their Dream Job posters using PowerPoint or similar slide show presentation programs like Google Slides.
> - Invite students to create videos using live actors, animation, voiceovers combined with images, etc.
> - Encourage students to use free downloadable poster-making programs.
> - If possible, allow students to upload their work to the school's website.
>
> Note that students should have the option to do a task on paper or digitally.

Wrap-up
Students compare posters and vote for their favorites.
- Invite students to vote for their favorite posters. There can be awards in various categories, e.g., best layout and design, best use of technology, best overall poster, etc.

➡ **Workbook p. 132, Activity 1 (Review)**

> 🗨 **Teaching Tip**
>
> **Displaying Students' Work**
>
> Teenagers are often motivated by having their work displayed for the rest of the class or the rest of the school to see. This may be especially true in the case of students who have fewer chances to shine or to have their achievements recognized in contexts such as formal tests and exams.

Review

Objectives
Students will be able to consolidate their understanding of the vocabulary and grammar learned in the unit.

Lesson 11 Student's Book p. 38

✔ **Homework Check!**
Workbook p. 132, Activity 1 (Review)

Answers
1 Write sentences. What are they doing?
Answers will vary.

Warm-up

Students play charades to practice professions and workplaces vocabulary.
• Invite students to play charades in small groups using the professions and workplaces that they have seen in this unit.

1 Read and match.
Students match professions with their descriptions.

Answers
1. c, 2. f, 3. e, 4. b, 5. d, 6. a

2 Unscramble the words.
Students unscramble words under each photo to practice workplaces vocabulary.

Answers
left to right airport, factory, fire station, hotel, salon, train station

3 Look and write sentences. What are they doing?
Students write sentences describing what people in photos are doing using the present continuous.

Answers
left to right They are dancing. They are walking. / They are crossing the street. He is baking. They are watching a movie.

Wrap-up

Students write personalized sentences using the present continuous.
• Ask students to write five sentences using the present continuous to describe people doing certain actions in certain places, for example, *My mom is working in her office.*
• Invite students to share their sentences with the rest of the class.

➡ **(No homework today.)**

Lesson 12 Student's Book p. 39

Warm-up
Students review the present continuous.
- Write on the board a series of prompts consisting of just a subject and a verb in its base form, for example, *she / study*. Elicit the sentence *She is studying.* to describe an action that is taking place now. Repeat with two or three other examples.

4 Correct the sentences.
Students rewrite the sentences with the correct form of the present continuous.

Answers
1. ~~I sitting~~ I <u>am</u> sitting on the bus.
2. ~~do~~ What are you <u>doing</u>?
3. ~~We not~~ We <u>are</u> not doing homework.
4. ~~have~~ Are you <u>having</u> lunch at school today?
5. ~~no~~ Jim is <u>not</u> playing basketball.
6. ~~watch~~ Are you <u>watching</u> TV?

5 Answer the questions about you.
Students answer questions in the present continuous.

Answers
Answers will vary.

6 Write the correct preposition.
Students label locations in a photo with the correct prepositions of place.

Answers
1. in, 2. at, 3. at, 4. at, 5. in, 6. on

? Big Question
Students are given the opportunity to revisit the Big Question and reflect on it.
- Tell students to turn to the unit opener on page 27 and look again at the photos, which show a variety of professions.
- Select one of the jobs, for example, the actor, and discuss with students whether this is the best job. Encourage students to think of reasons to support this idea and also to express any doubts or reservations based on parts of the job that are difficult, for example.
- Organize students into small groups and have them try to complete the following sentence in just 50 words: *In our opinion, the best job is…*
- As a whole-class activity, discuss students' ideas. Bring out the idea that, in fact, there is no one single job that is the best, since all jobs have positive and negative aspects. Encourage students to think about how an individual's preferences and personalities affect what the best job is for that person.

★ Scorecard
Hand out (and/or project) a *Scorecard*. Have students fill in their *Scorecards* for this unit.

⇒ Study for the unit test.

Teaching Tip
Reflecting on the Unit
At the end of a unit, ask students to reflect on what they enjoyed or did not enjoy so much, what they found easy, difficult, interesting, etc. Most importantly, ask students to identify things that they need to work more on so that they can improve.

3 Do we really need all this stuff?

Grammar	Vocabulary
Comparative and superlative adjectives: The man is <u>older</u> than the woman (comparative). This is the <u>cheapest</u> costume (superlative).	**Clothes:** belt, blouse, coat, dress, hat, jeans, jewelry, pants, scarf, shorts, skirt, sneakers, socks, sweater, T-shirt **Adjectives:** cheap, expensive, fast, funny, large, late, long, modern, old, polite, serious, short, small, tall

Reading	Listening
Skimming and scanning	Identifying specific information

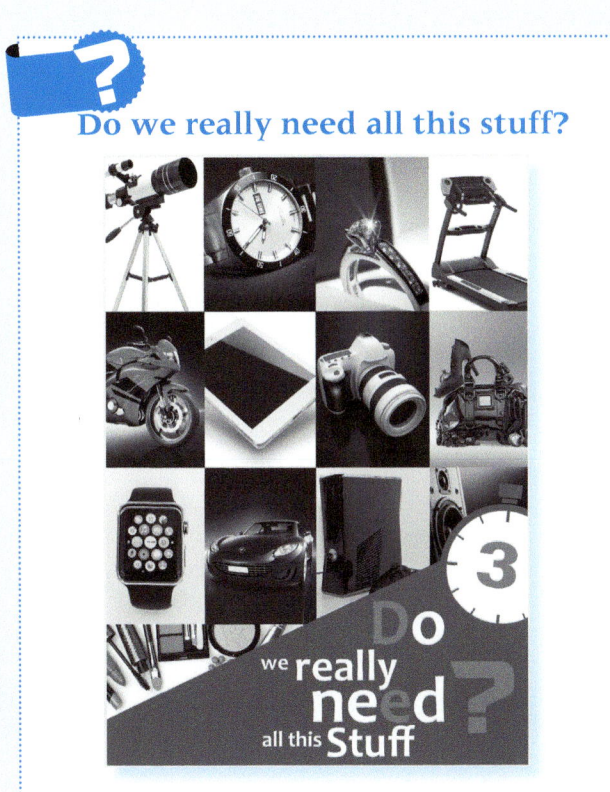

Do we really need all this stuff?

In the first lesson, read the unit title aloud and have students look carefully at the unit cover. Encourage them to think about the message in the picture. At the end of the unit, students will discuss the big question: *Do we really need all this stuff?*

Teaching Tip

Varying Seating Arrangements

Try different seating arrangements for different groups, for different types of learners and for different activities. If it is permitted in the place where you work, move the furniture around and try out new dynamics for learning. Put students' individual desks together to make one large table, or have students work around smaller tables in groups of four or five. Try different options to discover what works best in your specific situation.

Vocabulary

Objective
Students will be able to use **clothes** vocabulary and **adjectives** to talk about buying and wearing clothing.

Lesson 1 — Student's Book pp. 42 and 43

Warm-up

Students discuss their shopping habits.
- As a whole-class discussion, invite students to say how often they go shopping, if they enjoy going shopping, the kinds of things they buy, if they ever think they bought too much stuff, if they wish they could buy more things, etc.

1 🎧⁹ **Listen and circle the correct option.**

Students listen and circle the clothing items each speaker mentions.
- Draw students' attention to the *Guess What!* box. Read the information aloud and discuss with students places other than dictionaries where they can find new words.

Answers

1. hat, 2. T-shirt, 3. jeans, 4. coat, 5. scarf, 6. skirt, 7. dress, 8. shorts, 9. socks, 10. sneakers, 11. sweater, 12. pants

Audio Script

1. Look at this outfit. It's perfect for me! A hat, a T-shirt and some jeans.
2. These clothes are great for a cold morning: a coat, a scarf and a skirt.
3. I love formal clothes. This is a beautiful dress!
4. I need some shorts, some socks and a pair of sneakers for the gym.
5. This is my style of clothes: a comfortable sweater and a nice pair of pants.

2 Think Fast! What other clothes words do you know? Make a list.

Students do a five-minute timed challenge: they brainstorm more vocabulary for clothes.

> **Extension**
> Have students create labeled mini-posters of themselves wearing their favorite clothes. Invite students to present their posters to the rest of the class.

Wrap-up

Students create sales announcements for a clothing store.
- Tell students to create sales announcements, like the ones heard in department stores, informing customers about the discounts on certain items of clothing. Encourage them to use expressions from this page, e.g., *Today, all dresses and skirts are half price! 30% off all T-shirts and sweaters!*
- Invite students to read their sales announcements aloud.

➡ **Workbook p. 134, Activity 1**

Lesson 2 Student's Book p. 43

✔ **Homework Check!**

Workbook p. 134, Activity 1

Answers

1 Unscramble the words and find them in the word search.

1. dress, 2. hat, 3, jeans, 4. scarf, 5. shorts, 6. sneakers, 7. socks, 8. sweater

```
S F K E W M H G X D S
O W M S C A G W C R R
C G E C T M H E E T V
K J E A N S X K T D T
S H O R T S A D J X W
S C W F P E M M L T N
X R S Z N R R R Z F K
X H R S L D Y U H E I
```

Warm-up

Students play a word game with clothes vocabulary.
- Write clothing items on the board, with just the first letter and then dashes for the other missing letters, e.g. j _ _ _ _ (jeans). Have students guess the word.

3 🎧¹⁰ **Listen and write the clothes each person mentions.**
Students listen to four people talking about problems they sometimes have related to clothes and shoes and identify the specific items of clothing each speaker mentions.

Answers

1. dress, skirts, 2. sweaters, scarf, pants, 3. T-shirts, jeans, shorts, 4. shoes, sneakers

Audio Script

1. Lisa
   I love clothes, but I always have the same problem. We live in a village—it's miles away from the stores! I buy all my clothes online, but it's really difficult. If I see a dress online, the colors are often different in real life. The sizes are different too. In some stores, I'm a medium for skirts. In others, I'm a large. Ugh, I hate shopping online!
2. Ruth
   My mom and dad work, so I help around the house, but I always make the same mistakes with the laundry. Like I put the machine on too hot and I shrink my sweaters. They get really small and I can't wear them anymore. Or sometimes I put the wrong colors together. For instance, last week, I put my black scarf in with my dad's white pants and now his pants are gray. Oops!

3. Billy
   Suddenly, when I look in my closet, none of my clothes fit! I can't wear my T-shirts because they're too small. All my jeans are too tight. It's summer and it's 40 degrees Celsius, but I don't have any shorts in my size. I can't believe it!
4. Alberto
   You know what I hate? Shoe shopping. I love sneakers, but I have really big feet. Every time I go to the shoe store and ask to try some shoes on, they say, "What's your size?" I say I'm a size 12 and they act shocked. I mean, I'm not the only person in the world with feet that big!

4 🎧¹⁰ **Listen again and match the speakers to the problems.**
Students practice listening comprehension by identifying the problems each speaker discusses.

Answers

1. c, 2. a, 3. b, 4. d

5 Look and identify the events. What clothes can you wear for them?
Students match events with appropriate types of clothing.

Answers

1. Birthday party, Answers will vary. 2. Movie premiere, dress, pants, shirt, 3. Fun run, shorts, T-shirt, sneakers

Wrap-up

Students suggest appropriate clothing for a variety of events or occasions.
- Have students work in small groups and think of three places, events, etc. For each one, ask them to write a list of appropriate clothing, footwear, etc.
- Have students share their lists with the rest of the class.

➡ **Workbook p. 134, Activities 2 and 3**

Grammar

Objective
Students will be able to use **comparatives** and **superlatives** to compare costumes.

Lesson 3 — Student's Book p. 44

✔ **Homework Check!**
Workbook p. 134, Activities 2 and 3

Answers
2 Cross out the word that doesn't belong. Explain why it's different.
1. jeans, A scarf and a sweater are worn when it's cold. / A scarf and sweater are worn on the upper half of the body. 2. hat, A hat is worn on the head. / A blouse and a T-shirt are worn on the chest. 3. sneakers, Sneakers are worn on the feet. / Jeans and pants are worn on the legs. 4. shorts, Shorts are worn when it's warm. / A coat and a scarf are worn when it's cold. 5. jeans, Jeans are worn on the legs. / Socks and sneakers are worn on the feet.
3 Look and complete with as many clothes words as you can.
1. a hat, a T-shirt, shorts and sneakers, 2. a hat, a scarf, a coat, jeans and sneakers

Warm-up
Students brainstorm adjectives for describing items of clothing.
- Organize students into pairs and have them think of adjectives that can describe items of clothing (*large, small, long, short, cheap, etc.*).
- Compile a list of adjectives on the board.

1 🎧 **Read the comic and complete the sentences. Then listen and check.**
Students read the comic and complete sentences with the correct comparative adjective forms.
- Draw students' attention to the **Comparative** box and read the information aloud.

Answers
1. smaller, 2. larger, 3. more expensive, 4. cheaper, 5. more polite

Audio Script
1. The chicken mask is smaller than the dog mask.
2. The dog mask is larger than the chicken mask.
3. The stormtrooper helmet is more expensive than the robot mask. 4. The robot mask is cheaper than the stormtrooper helmet. 5. The woman is more polite than the man.

2 Look and write the comparatives.
Students write the comparative forms of a selection of adjectives.

Answers
1. faster, 2. older, 3. funnier, 4. more serious, 5. shorter, 6. more modern, 7. longer, 8. later

Extension
Students create informative posters about comparative adjectives.
- Have students work in small groups.
- Ask students to list the spelling rules for comparative adjectives and encourage them to think of ways to illustrate the rules.
- Have students create posters explaining the spelling rules, and display their posters in the classroom.

Wrap-up
Students play Comparatives Bingo.
- Prepare Bingo cards with nine squares on each card and a comparative adjective in each square.
- To play, read aloud a series of adjectives in their base form and have students cross out the corresponding comparative form when they hear it. The first student to get a line of three (vertically, horizontally, or diagonally) calls out Bingo! and wins the game.

➡ **Workbook p. 135, Activities 1 and 2**

🐝 Teaching Tip
Modeling Language
When giving the comparative form of an adjective, use the comparative in a sentence. For example, say *The comparative form of funny is funnier: The book was funnier than the movie.* This will help emphasize the use of *than*.

Lesson 4 — Student's Book p. 45

✔ **Homework Check!**

Workbook p. 135, Activities 1 and 2

Answers

1 Complete the sentences with the comparative form of the adjectives.
1. bigger, 2. hotter, 3. farther, 4. worse, 5. thinner

2 Correct one mistake in each sentence.
1. ~~more far~~ The mall is <u>farther</u> than the school.
2. ~~more fast~~ A horse is <u>faster</u> than a dog.
3. ~~heavyer~~ Your suitcase is <u>heavier</u> than my bag.
4. ~~more good~~ Yoga is <u>better</u> than swimming.
5. ~~intelligenter~~ You're <u>more intelligent</u> than him!

Warm-up

Students share experiences and ideas about costume parties.
- Tell students to look at the three costumes at the top of the page and to say what they think the people are dressed up as.
- Invite students to share stories of costume parties that they have attended and the costumes that they have worn.

3 Read the e-mail and complete the questions. Then answer them.

Students read an e-mail, complete questions about it with superlative forms and answer the questions.
- Draw students' attention just to the **Superlatives** box and read the information aloud.

Answers

1. the most expensive, the stormtrooper, 2. the funniest, the bear, 3. the cheapest, the robot, 4. the best, Answers will vary.

4 Complete with a comparative or superlative adjective.

Students determine whether the comparative or the superlative form of given adjectives best completes each sentence and write the appropriate form of each adjective.

Answers

1. the most practical, 2. taller than, 3. funnier than, 4. the coolest

Wrap-up

Students write sentences using comparative and superlative adjectives.
- Elicit adjectives from students and write them on the board. Tell students to choose six adjectives and to write three sentences using the comparative form and three sentences using the superlative form.
- Invite students to share their sentences with the rest of the class.

➡ **Workbook p. 136, Activities 3 and 4**

Reading and Listening

Objectives
Students will be able to skim and scan a text. They will also be able to identify specific information when listening.

Lesson 5 — Student's Book pp. 46 and 47

✔ **Homework Check!**
Workbook p. 136, Activities 3 and 4

Answers
3 Unscramble the superlative sentences in your notebook.
1. Tokyo is the largest city on the planet. 2. Jupiter is the biggest planet in the Solar System. 3. *Avatar* is the most successful movie of all time. 4. Mount Everest in the highest mountain on the planet. 5. Malaria is the most dangerous disease on Earth. 6. The world's shortest woman is 0.62 meters tall.
4 Rewrite the sentences using the superlative.
1. Our classroom is the largest classroom in the school. 2. My little brother is the youngest kid in his kindergarten. 3. The hot chocolate is the most expensive drink in the restaurant. 4. Monday is the busiest day in school. 5. March is the wettest month. 6. The stormtrooper costume is the best one.

Warm-up
Students exchange information about their favorite places to eat.
- Organize students into pairs and ask them to share information about places that they like to eat, such as restaurants, fast food places, outdoor markets, etc.
- As a whole-class activity, discuss students' ideas.

1 Think Fast! What's on the page? How do you know?
Students do a one-minute timed challenge: they skim a text to get an initial main idea of its content.
- Draw students' attention to the *Be Strategic!* box and read the information aloud.

Answer
A menu

2 Scan the menu and answer the questions.
Students scan a text carefully to obtain specific information.

Answers
1. Yes, you can. 2. A milkshake is $3.00 and a piece of cheesecake is $8.50, for a total of $11.50. 3. The buffalo wings are the most expensive. 4. You can get a green salad for $11.90 and hot or iced tea for $2.00, for a total of $13.90. 5. Yes, you can get cod and rice. 6. You need $11.90 for the green salad, $25.90 for the veggie cheeseburger and $2.00 for hot or iced tea, for a total of $39.80.

Extension
Students create their own menus.
- Have students form small groups and decide on the type of restaurant they would like to create a menu for.
- Have students create their menus, including food, drinks and prices.
- Encourage students to share their menus with the class.

Wrap-up
Students create word puzzles with food and drink vocabulary.
- Invite students to create wordsearch puzzles or crossword puzzles (the crossword clues can be simple pictures) using food and drink items from the menu on these pages.
- Have students share their puzzles with other students.

➡ Workbook p. 137, Activities 1 and 2

Teaching Tip
Managing Fast Finishers
Some students complete activities more quickly than others, so it's a good idea to have a few extra activities on hand, otherwise these students may become bored and disruptive. One set of activities designed for fast finishers are the *Just for Fun* pages. Students can work on these individually and then check their answers in the back of the Student's Book. The *Just for Fun* activities for this unit are on page 54.

Lesson 6   Student's Book pp. 46 and 47

> ✔ **Homework Check!**
> Workbook p. 137, Activities 1 and 2
> **Answers**
> **1 Read the text quickly (skimming) and mark (✓) the correct topic.**
> breakfast
> **2 Read and find (scanning) one breakfast…**
> 1. *tapsilog*, 2. *nihari*, 3. the full English breakfast

Warm-up
Students discuss their food preferences.
- Ask students to look again at the menu and to say what they would choose.

3 🎧¹² **Listen and circle Paul's choices on the menu.**
Students listen to a conversation to obtain specific information.

Answers
Green Salad, Cod and Rice, Ice Cream

Audio Script
Mom: So Paul, what's your decision? The nachos right? They're tastier than the salad.
Paul: I don't know. Nachos have a lot of salt and they also have a thick cheesy sauce. Dairy products contain a lot of fat.
Mom: Well, I'm having the nachos.
Paul: It's the green salad for me.
Dad: Please yourself, Paul. I'm having the Caesar salad.
Mom: Now the main course. A juicy steak?
Dad: Mmm, yes!
Paul: Uh… Steak isn't a great choice.
Dad: Why not?
Paul: Doctors say it's OK to eat a little red meat, but that steak is half a kilo! The fish is healthier than the steak.
Mom: Fish?
Paul: The cod and rice. Fish has lots of vitamins and oils.
Dad: And the veggie burger?
Paul: The problem with the burger is the French fries. Fries have a lot of fat. I'm having the fish.
Mom: Dessert?
Paul: Well, obviously the fruit salad is better than the ice cream, but…
Mom and dad: But?
Paul: I want the ice cream! I love it!
Mom: Me too.
Dad: Make that three.
Mom: And to drink?
Paul: Sodas are the worst drinks. They contain lots of sugar.
Mom: Yeah. Water is fine.

4 🎧¹² **Listen again and choose the correct options.**
Students listen for specific information and choose the correct options to complete the sentences.

Answers
1. salt, 2. red, 3. French fries, 4. better, 5. sugar

Stop and Think! Critical Thinking
How do you choose what to buy in a restaurant?
- Organize students into small groups and have them brainstorm ideas about how they decide what food to order. (If necessary, write some ideas on the board to get them started.)
- Invite groups to share their ideas with the rest of the class.

Wrap-up
Students role-play restaurant scenes.
- Invite students to work in pairs or threes role-playing similar restaurant scenes.

➡ **Workbook p. 137, Activities 3 and 4**

Preparing for the Next Lesson
Ask students to watch an introduction to China: goo.gl/SPdQ.

Culture

Objectives
Students will be able to discuss different ways people celebrate birthdays and the value of gift-giving.

Lesson 7 — Student's Book pp. 48 and 49

> ✔ **Homework Check!**
> Workbook p. 137, Activities 3 and 4
> **Answers**
> **3 Read again and circle *T* (True) or *F* (False).**
> 1. F (The information on breakfasts in the Philippines and in Pakistan doesn't mention drinks.), 2. T, 3. T, 4. T
> **4 Describe a breakfast in your country or in your family.**
> Answers will vary.

▶ 50 **Warm-up**

Students share general knowledge about various aspects of China.
- As a whole-class activity, invite students to share what they know about China (its geography, its population, its culture, its history, its food, its economy, its language, its customs, etc.).
- Write ideas on the board. If students are not completely sure about something, mark the point with a question mark.

1 Complete the text with the superlative form of the adjectives.
Students practice superlative adjectives in a reading text.
Answers
1. the oldest, 2. the most important, 3. the biggest, 4. the largest, 5. the richest

2 Look at the pictures on the cell phone. How are they related?
Students discuss what event a series of personal photos shows.
Answers
They all have to do with a birthday celebration in China.

Extension
Students prepare a gallery of photos.
- Invite students to prepare a group of photos to show how they celebrate birthdays in their own country.
- They can include details about parties, presents, customs, places, etc.

Wrap-up
Students arrange themselves in a line by date of birth.
- Set a time limit of, say, two minutes and challenge the whole class to stand in a line from the youngest to the oldest. In order to complete the task, students will have to ask each other their dates of birth, including the year.

▶ **(No homework today.)**

> 🎓 **Teaching Tip**
> **Encouraging Curiosity about Other Cultures**
> When students travel abroad in the future, they will meet native speakers of English but also a great number of non-native speakers from a wide variety of countries. In this way, learning English opens windows onto many other cultures. Encourage students to be curious about people from other places and to always be sensitive to other people's cultures and traditions.

Lesson 8   Student's Book pp. 48 and 49

Warm-up

Students review factual information about China.

- Write on the board a series of statements about China, some true and some false, for example:
  1. China is officially known as The People's Republic of China. 2. China is the largest country by area in the world. 3. The capital of China is Beijing. 4. China hosted the 2012 Olympic Games., etc.

- Ask students to identify and correct the false statements.

Answers

1. T, 2. F (China is the third largest, after Russia and Canada.), 3. T, 4. F (China hosted the 2008 Olympic Games; the UK hosted the 2012 Olympic Games.)

3 🎧¹³ Unscramble the words and complete the sentences. Listen and check.

Students unscramble words in order to complete sentences.

Answers

1. birthday, 2. cats, 3. money, 4. cake

Audio Script

BARRY: You look happy today, Jing!
JING: I am happy today. It's my birthday.
BARRY: Happy birthday! Are you getting lots of gifts?
JING: No, not really. In China, we don't get lots of gifts. I normally only get one.
BARRY: One present! What is it?
JING: It's a book about cats. I love them! And my grandparents always give me some money. They give it in a red envelope. That's a tradition in China.
BARRY: Do you have a birthday cake?
JING: Yes! I have a cake with 12 candles for me this year. And we eat special noodles. In fact, it's one long noodle. The longest noodle on earth! This special noodle represents long life.
BARRY: Wow! That's so cool!
JING: Yes, it is! I'm very happy with my birthday gifts.

4 🎧¹³ Correct the false information. Then listen again to check.

Students correct false information and then confirm their answers by listening to the audio again.

Answers

1. ~~toys~~ gifts, 2. ~~a card~~ money, 3. ~~14~~ 12, 4. ~~happiness~~ long life, 5. ~~sad~~ happy

5 Mark (✓) the best summary.

Students select the best sentence to summarize a text.

Answer

2. In China, birthday gifts have a special meaning.

Stop and Think! Critical Thinking

What does it mean to give a gift?

- Organize students into small groups and have them brainstorm ideas about what it means to give a gift to someone and, also, what it means to receive a gift from someone else. If necessary, write some ideas on the board to get them started.

- Invite groups to share their ideas with the rest of the class.

Wrap-up

Students recap what they learned from the reading and listening texts.

- Tell students to briefly summarize (in three or four sentences) what they learned about birthday celebrations in China.

▶ **(No homework today.)**

Project

Objective
Students will be able to create a bulletin board with money-saving tips.

Lesson 9   Student's Book pp. 50 and 51

Warm-up

Students discuss shopping.
- As a whole-class activity, ask students through a simple show-of-hands vote who likes shopping, who consider themselves to be smart shoppers, who is careful with their money, etc.

1 Unscramble the sentences. Which are true for you?
Students unscramble sentences as part of a self-test.

Answers
1. I do jobs at home to earn some money. 2. I never have any money! 3. I always save some money for emergencies. 4. My parents give me some money every week. 5. I always spend all of my money.

2 Write the letters of the tips on the bulletin board.
Students match pieces of advice with the correct headings.

Answers
1. d, 2. c, 3. e, 4. a, 5. f, 6. b

Wrap-up

Students discuss shopping tips that they are familiar with.
- Review the information on the bulletin board and invite students to comment on their own experience of these strategies employed by stores to try to persuade shoppers to buy more things and spend more money. Encourage them to add any ideas of their own.

> **Teaching Tip**
> **Encouraging Critical Thinking**
> Encourage students to think critically. Try to help students develop the habit of not accepting a text such as an advertisement at face value, but rather, of thinking about who wrote the text, why the person wrote the text, and the effect that the author wants the text to have on a reader, etc.

Lesson 10   Student's Book pp. 50 and 51

Warm-up
Students review the techniques that stores use to make shoppers buy / spend more.
- Tell students to imagine that they are managers of clothing stores or supermarkets. Have them write three techniques that they can use in order to encourage shoppers to buy more things and/or spend more money in their store.
- Invite students to share their ideas with the rest of the class.

3 Look at the highlighted words in the board. Choose the correct option.
Students practice finding out the meaning of a word through context.

Answers
1. b, 2. c, 3. a, 4. c, 5. c, 6. b

4 Design your own bulletin board with money-saving tips. Present it to the class.
Students design and create a bulletin board with money-saving tips.
- Have students design and create their bulletin boards, using the model on these pages as a guide if they wish.
- Have them look for photos that they can use or have them create their own pictures.
- Encourage them to work on the format, the design and the layout of their bulletin board (the overall look and how the text and images combine together).
- Once students have written their texts, ask them to check them carefully for spelling, punctuation and grammar.

The Digital Touch
To incorporate digital media in the project, suggest one or more of the following:
- Have students present their bulletin boards using PowerPoint or similar slide show presentation programs like Google Slides.
- Invite students to create videos using live actors, animation, voiceovers combined with images, etc.
- Encourage students to use free downloadable poster-making programs for their bulletin boards.
- If possible, allow students to upload their work to the school's website.

Note that students should have the option to do a task on paper or digitally.

Wrap-up
Students compare bulletin boards and vote for their favorites.
- Invite students to vote for their favorite bulletin boards. There can be awards in various categories, e.g., best layout and design, best use of technology, best overall board, etc.

➡ **Workbook p. 136, Activity 1 (Review)**

Review

Objective
Students will be able to consolidate their understanding of the vocabulary and grammar learned in the unit.

Lesson 11   Student's Book p. 52

> ✔ **Homework Check!**
> Workbook p. 136, Activity 1 (Review)
> **Answers**
> **1 Complete about you.**
> Answers will vary.

Warm-up

Students play Hangman to practice clothes vocabulary.
- Invite students to play Hangman in two teams, using the items of clothing, footwear and accessories that they have seen in this unit.

▶ 54

1 Find 12 words in the word snake.
Students practice clothes vocabulary in a puzzle.

Answers
sneakers, hat, blouse, shorts, coat, scarf, jeans, dress, sweater, pants, socks

2 Cross out the word that doesn't belong in each sentence.
Students practice clothes vocabulary by identifying the odd one out of a group.

Answers
1. some shorts, 2. a coat, 3. blouse, 4. jeans, 5. dresses, 6. a dress, 7. skirt, 8. sneakers

3 Complete with the comparative form of the adjectives.
Students practice comparative adjectives in a sentence completion exercise.

Answers
1. more modern, 2. more serious, 3. younger, 4. taller, 5. older, 6. funnier, 7. smaller, 8. longer

4 Write the comparative forms and number the pictures.
Students give the comparative forms of adjectives and match them with the appropriate picture.

Answers
1. more beautiful, 2. cheaper, 3. more dangerous, 4. more difficult, 5. slower, 6. stronger; *left to right* 6, 5, 1, 2, 4, 3

Wrap-up

Students compile a comparative adjectives chart.
- Ask students to work in small groups compiling a comprehensive chart containing a large number of adjectives with their comparative forms. They should be sure to cover all the different types of adjective and all the spelling variants.
- Display students' work around the classroom.

▶ **(No homework today.)**

Lesson 12   Student's Book p. 53

Warm-up
Students share information about world records that they know.
- Invite students to share any world records that they know, especially any unusual records.
- Write them up on the board and, if possible, verify the accuracy and authenticity of the records by consulting reliable sources of information.

5 Complete with the superlative form of the adjectives.
Students review superlative adjectives in a reading and sentence completion activity.

Answers
1. oldest, 2. most expensive, 3. tallest, 4. the most popular, 5. The longest

6 Choose the correct options to complete the sentences.
Students choose between the comparative and the superlative form of an adjective to complete sentences.

Answers
1. most embarrassing, 2. more difficult, 3. the shortest, best, 4. older, 5. heavier, 6. strictest, 7. friendlier, 8. thickest

Big Question
Students are given the opportunity to revisit the Big Question and reflect on it.
- Tell students to turn to the unit opener on page 41 and look again at the photo, which shows a lot of products.
- Ask students what kinds of stores they think the different products can be found in. Encourage them to speculate about various possibilities.
- Ask students about times when they bought something, perhaps on impulse, that they did not really need. Ask them how they felt about it afterwards.
- As a whole-class activity, debate the idea that our society in general has become too interested in buying things even when we do not really need them.
- Invite students to suggest ways in which people can become more responsible shoppers.

Scorecard
Hand out (and/or project) a *Scorecard*. Have students fill in their *Scorecards* for this unit.

Study for the unit test.

Teaching Tip
Summarizing the Unit
At the end of a unit, invite various students to give a brief summary of the key points that were covered and to say what they learned.

4 How do you protect the planet?

Grammar

Countable and uncountable nouns: We have <u>carrots</u> and <u>lettuce</u>.

Quantifiers: *a lot of, some, a little, a few, any*: <u>How much</u> coffee is there? There's <u>some</u> coffee. There's <u>a little</u> milk, but there isn't <u>any</u> sugar.

How much, How many

Vocabulary

Food: apple, bread, carrot, flour, lettuce, lime, milk, onion, orange, salami, strawberry, sugar, potato, tomato

Writing

Organizing ideas in paragraphs

Speaking

Interviewing a classmate

How do you protect the planet?

In the first lesson, read the unit title aloud and have students look carefully at the unit cover. Encourage them to think about the message in the picture. At the end of the unit, students will discuss the big question: *How do you protect the planet?*

Teaching Tip

Explaining the Importance of Mistakes

Some students worry about making mistakes, and this can affect their confidence and their willingness to participate in class. Explain to students that mistakes are an inevitable and necessary part of language learning. Explain that they can learn a lot from identifying and analyzing a mistake and comparing it with the correct word or form. It is at these moments that a lot of learning takes place.

Vocabulary

Objective
Students will be able to use **food** and **containers** vocabulary to talk about gardening and food.

Lesson 1 Student's Book p. 56

Warm-up
Students brainstorm ways to protect the environment.
- Bring a ball or other soft throwable object to class. Have students stand up and form a circle.
- Tell students that you will throw the ball to each other; whoever gets the ball shouts out a way to protect the environment. Before starting, give students examples like *don't litter* or *turn off the lights*.
- Play as long as time permits and students are engaged.

1 Read and classify the vegetables and fruits.
Students practice fruits and vegetables vocabulary in a classifying activity.

Answers
Vegetables carrots, lettuce, onions, potatoes
Fruits apples, limes, oranges, strawberries

2 Think Fast! Can you think of five more fruits and vegetables?
Students do a three-minute timed challenge: they add more fruits and vegetables to their lists.

Answers
Answers will vary.

3 🎧14 Listen and write the quantities in the table. Who won the competition?
Students listen to a conversation and identify specific information.

Answers
Hot Potatoes 1. carrots, 2 kilos, 2. potatoes, 3 kilos, 3. lettuce, 0 kilos, 4. onions, 2 kilos
Go Bananas 1. apples, 1 kilo, 2. limes, 0 kilos, 3. oranges, 1 kilo, 4. strawberries, 0 kilos
The Hot Potatoes won the competition.

Audio Script
PRINCIPAL: Thank you, everyone. It's time to announce the winner of the school gardening competition. First, let's hear from Mr. Steele, leader of the Hot Potatoes. Mr. Steele, tell us about your team.
MR. STEELE: This year, the Hot Potatoes are growing vegetables. What a year. It never rains, so we water the plants every day. Luckily, we have some veggies!
PRINCIPAL: What do you have?
MR. STEELE: We have two kilos of carrots and three kilos of potatoes.
PRINCIPAL: That's wonderful! How about the lettuce?
MR. STEELE: We don't have any lettuce. The caterpillars love them!
PRINCIPAL: And the onions?
MR. STEELE: We have two kilos of onions. The fertilizer is important because plants need nutrients.
PRINCIPAL: Now, let's hear from Ms. Dance and the Go Bananas team.
MS. DANCE: OK! We're growing fruits. It's not easy.
PRINCIPAL: Do you have any apples?
MS. DANCE: Yes, we have one kilo of apples.
PRINCIPAL: Do you have any limes?
MS. DANCE: No, we don't have any limes. I think people pick our limes off the tree. They steal them.
PRINCIPAL: Oh no! Oranges?
MS. DANCE: We have one kilo of oranges.
PRINCIPAL: And your last fruit. What was it?
MS. DANCE: Strawberries. But we don't have any strawberries.
PRINCIPAL: No strawberries? What's the problem?
MS. DANCE: The weeds! The weeds grow and the strawberries don't! They're everywhere.
PRINCIPAL: So that's it. The winner of this year's school gardening competition... the Hot Potatoes!!!

Wrap-up
Students role-play the conversation about the Garden Project competition to practice using *there is / are*, *some*, *any* and food vocabulary.
- Students form pairs. Student A will be the principal, and Student B will be Mr. Steele. Tell students to recreate the interview using the tables they completed on page 56.
- Then have students switch roles: Student B will be the principal and Student A will be Ms. Dance.

▶ **Workbook p. 138, Activities 1 and 2**

Lesson 2 Student's Book p. 57

✔ **Homework Check!**

Workbook p. 138, Activities 1 and 2

Answers

1 Find and write seven types of food.

O	R	A	N	G	E	V	L	Y	P
A	R	Y	V	Y	H	L	I	O	O
P	Q	J	J	D	U	E	M	N	T
P	Y	Z	X	D	W	T	E	I	A
L	C	A	R	R	O	T	Z	O	T
E	P	T	F	K	U	U	J	N	O
O	Q	X	H	V	Z	C	T	H	Q
S	T	R	A	W	B	E	R	R	Y

1. apple, 2. carrot, 3. lettuce. 4. lime, 5. onion, 6. potato, 7. strawberry

2 Guess what fruit or vegetable each picture suggests.

1. orange, 2. lime, 3. carrot, 4. strawberry, 5. lettuce, 6. apple, 7. onion

Warm-up

Students play a quick game and then talk about growing fruits and vegetables.

- Write the first letter of a fruit or vegetable followed by dashes for the remaining letters on the board, e.g., p _ _ _ _ _ (potato). Students call out the words.
- Ask *What grows on trees?* (limes, oranges, apples) *What grows in the ground?* (strawberries, potatoes, lettuce, onions, carrots).
- Have students tell you what (if anything) they grow in their gardens at home.

4 Match the recommendations using the picture.

Students match recommendations with actions shown in a picture.

- Ask students to look at the picture. Elicit that it shows people carrying out various tasks related to growing fruits and vegetables.

Answers

1. c, 2. h, 3. f, 4. g, 5. b, 6. e, 7. d, 8. a

5 Cross out the word that doesn't belong in each sentence.

Students read sentences and identify the word that does not make sense in the sentence.

- Draw students' attention to the **Guess What!** box. Read the information aloud and discuss the expression *a green thumb*. Ask students why we say *green thumb* (because plants are green). Ask students if they consider themselves to have green thumbs and, if so, why.

Answers

1. weeds, 2. Earthworms, 3. Snails, 4. caterpillars, 5. fertilizers, 6. seeds

Wrap-up

Students create spider diagrams to record verb-noun collocations.

- Have students form small groups to create spider diagrams showing common collocations, for example, nouns that can follow the verb *water* (plants, tomatoes, trees) or the verb *pick* (oranges, strawberries).

▶ **Workbook pp. 138 and 139, Activities 3 and 4**

Grammar

Objective
Students will be able to use **countable and uncountable nouns** and **quantifiers** to talk about food, containers, waste and gardening.

Lesson 3 — Student's Book pp. 58 and 59

✔ **Homework Check!**
Workbook pp. 138 and 139, Activities 3 and 4

Answers
3 Match the parts of the sentences.
1. e, 2. a, 3. h, 4. b, 5. g, 6. d, 7. f
4 Correct the false information in the sentences.
[Accept all reasonable answers.]
1. ~~oranges~~ You dig <u>potatoes / carrots</u> out of the ground. 2. ~~Potatoes~~ <u>Fruits</u> have seeds. 3. ~~dogs~~ You give fertilizer to <u>plants</u>. 4. ~~carrots~~ You pick <u>apples /oranges / limes</u> off a tree. 5. ~~fast~~ Snails move very <u>slowly</u> in the garden. 6. ~~trees~~ Earthworms live in <u>dirt</u>.

Warm-up

Students try to guess how much garbage they produce each day.
- Draw students' attention to the photo of recycling bins in Activity 2. Ask *How much garbage do you produce every day?*
- Tell them that according to the US Environmental Protection Agency, each US citizen produces on average 4–5 pounds of trash daily.

1 🎧¹⁵ **Listen and label the objects on the table.**
Students listen and label various objects in photos (items of food and containers for food).

Audio Script
1. Bags — B-A-G-S
2. Bread — B-R-E-A-D
3. Milk — M-I-L-K
4. Flour — F-L-O-U-R
5. Boxes — B-O-X-E-S
6. Bottles — B-O-T-T-L-E-S
7. Sugar — S-U-G-A-R
8. Caps — C-A-P-S
9. Dishes — D-I-S-H-E-S
10. Salami — S-A-L-A-M-I

2 Write the words in the correct recycling bin.
Students sort food and containers vocabulary into categories according to how the items are collected as trash.

Answers
food bread, flour, sugar, salami, *paper* bags, *bottles and cans* bottles, caps, *mixed* boxes, dishes

Extension
Students discuss recycling services.
- Organize students into small groups and invite them to discuss and comment on the recycling services, if any, offered in their school, their parents' places of work, public spaces in their community, etc.

Wrap-up
Students relate types of food to certain types of container.
- Write on the board the following types of containers as the headings of three columns: *Bags, Boxes, Bottles*.
- Form three teams. Have students line up in their teams. One student at a time from each team will run to the board and write a food item in the team's column. For example, *cereal* could go in the *Boxes* column.
- After writing a food item under the column, each student sits back down. The team who are all seated first wins.

▶ **(No homework today.)**

Lesson 4
Student's Book pp. 58 and 59

Warm-up
Students share information about recycled and recyclable products.
- Students form small groups. Tell groups to look among their school equipment / supplies for things that are or that can be recycled and make a list.
- Set a stopwatch for three minutes.
- After three minutes, have groups share with the class what they found. The group that finds the most items wins.

3 Look at the items in Activity 1 and choose the correct option.
Students practice countable and uncountable nouns as they select options to complete sentences about quantities of items in the photo.
- Draw students' attention to the *Uncountables* and *Countables* boxes. Emphasize the idea that liquids and foods like salt, sugar, etc. cannot be counted. When we refer to these items, we use a container (e.g., a bottle) or a unit of measurement (e.g., liters).

Answers

1. a little, 2. much, 3. a lot of, 4. isn't any, 5. a little, 6. any

4 Look at the table again and complete the chart.
Students sort food items by quantity.
- Tell students to look at the items on the table at the top of the previous page. Have students work alone or in pairs completing the exercise. Check and discuss answers. If necessary, review the information in the boxes about uncountable and countable nouns.

Answers

a few bags, bottles, boxes, *some* sugar, bread, caps, *a lot of* flour, dishes

5 Unscramble the sentences.
Students practice quantity expressions in an unscrambling exercise.
- Have students work alone or in pairs completing the exercise. Check answers by having students read the unscrambled sentences aloud.

Answers

1. There's a little milk for the cake. 2. How much oil is there? 3. I can see some flour in the bag. 4. There are a lot of dishes on the table. 5. How many boxes do you have? 6. There aren't any tomatoes.

Stop and Think! Critical Thinking
What things do you recycle?
- Organize students into small groups and have them exchange information about what items they recycle. (If necessary, write some ideas on the board to get them started.)
- Invite groups to share their comments with the rest of the class.

Wrap-up
Students create posters about quantity expressions.
- Invite students to work in groups preparing posters that explain the quantity expressions that we use with countable and uncountable nouns.

➠ **Workbook pp. 139 and 140, Activities 1–3**

Teaching Tip
Using Realia
To show the difference between countable and uncountable nouns in a way that is memorable, bring to class a small amount of uncooked rice, for example, and show how difficult, and absurd, it is to count rice.

Writing and Speaking

Objectives
Students will be able to organize ideas in paragraphs. They will also be able to interview a classmate.

Lesson 5 Student's Book pp. 60 and 61

✔ **Homework Check!**
Workbook pp. 139 and 140, Activities 1–3
Answers
1 Complete the questions with *much* or *many*.
1. many, 2. much, 3. many, 4. many, 5. much
2 Choose the correct option for each picture.
1. a little sugar, 2. a lot of chocolate, 3. a little ice cream, 4. some meat, 5. some tea
3 Choose the correct option to complete the newspaper story.
1. a few, 2. some, 3. some, 4. some, 5. any, 6. a lot of, 7. a little, 8. a few, 9. a little

62 Warm-up
Students talk about pets.
- In small groups, tell students to discuss what kinds of animals students (or their friends, neighbors, relatives) have as pets.
- As a whole class, have groups tell you the pets they discussed. Have students raise their hands if they know someone who has each pet. See which pets are most common.

1 Match the descriptions with the paragraphs in the essay.
Students identify the different parts of an essay.
Answers
1. d, 2. c, 3. a, 4. b

2 Match the descriptions and the pictures.
Students match descriptions of animals with pictures.
Answers
1. e, 2. d, 3. f, 4. a, 5. b, 6. c

Extension
Students discuss animals that can and cannot be pets.
- Organize students into small groups and have them draw up two lists: one of animals that can be kept as pets and the other of animals that cannot be kept as pets.
- Ask students to compare their lists with those of other groups and to discuss any differences of opinion.

Wrap-up
Students play a guessing game with animals.
- Invite students to play a guessing game in small groups. Two small groups play together, with each group as one team.
- Give teams five minutes to write five short descriptions of five animals.
- One team reads aloud one of their descriptions and the other team has to guess the animal.
- Then teams switch roles. The team that guesses the right animal correctly in a maximum of two tries gets a point.
- Teams go back and forth reading and guessing until both have read all five of their descriptions. The team with the most points at the end wins.

➡ **Workbook p. 141, Activities 1 and 2**

Lesson 6 Student's Book pp. 60 and 61

> ✔ **Homework Check!**
> Workbook p. 141, Activities 1 and 2
> **Answers**
> **1 Read the blog and mark (✓) three differences in the original plan.**
> Paragraph 1: About me, Paragraph 3: A famous fish from Puerto Rico, Paragraph 5: A scary snake from Puerto Rico
> **2 Correct the false information in the sentences.**
> 1. ~~13~~ There are 80 types of birds in Puerto Rico. 2. ~~dogs~~ Bats eat the island's mosquitoes. 3. ~~insects~~ Manatees are large mammals. 4. ~~butterfly~~ The red and green Puerto Rican parrot is an endangered species.

Warm-up
Students create stories in groups.
- Students form small groups. Assign each group an animal mentioned in the unit (in the Student's Book or the Workbook).
- Give each student a slip of paper. Tell groups to write a group story with the animal you assign them as the hero. Have groups decide who will write the first sentence. Then student A passes his/her slip with the first sentence to student B, who writes the second sentence on his/her slip of paper, and then passes both slips to Student C, and so on until every group member has written a sentence, building the story as they go.
- Then have groups mix up their slips of paper and trade them with another group. Each group tries to recreate the sequence of the other group's story by putting the slips in order. When they finish, have groups check each other's work and say if the sequence of the story was correct.

3 Write an essay about your favorite animal.
Students write essays about their favorite animals.
- Draw students' attention to the **Be Strategic!** box. Read the information aloud and make sure that students understand the importance of planning their writing.
- Invite students to share their finished work with the rest of the class.

4 Write the questions. Interview your partner.
Students write interview questions and use them to interview classmates.
Answers
1. What is your favorite animal? 2. What does it look like? 3. Where does it live? 4. What does it eat? 5. Is it an endangered species? 6. Is it a popular pet? 7. Why is it your favorite?

Extension
Students create information posters about an endangered species.
- Have students work in small groups.
- Tell students to look for information about an animal that is an endangered species.
- Have students create posters explaining what the animal looks like, what it eats, and why it is endangered. Display the posters around the classroom.

Stop and Think! Critical Thinking
Why are animals important to our world?
- Organize students into small groups and have them brainstorm ideas about why animals are important. (If necessary, write some ideas on the board to get them started.)
- Invite groups to share their ideas with the rest of the class.

Wrap-up
Students review vocabulary related to animals.
- Set students quick-fire challenges to practice vocabulary of animal body parts (wings, tail, etc.) and verbs describing movement (fly, swim, run, climb, etc.) Say, for example, *Name three animals that have wings. Name three animals that have fur*.

➡ **Workbook p. 141, Activity 1 (Writing)**

Preparing for the Next Lesson
Ask students to watch an introduction to Sweden's recycling program: goo.gl/yY8zjW.

Culture

Objectives
Students will be able to learn about innovations in recycling and to develop awareness of the importance of recycling.

Lesson 7   Student's Book pp. 62 and 63

> ✔ **Homework Check!**
> Workbook p. 141, Activity 1 (Writing)
> Answers
> 1 Write a similar blog.
> Answers will vary.

Warm-up
Students make some guesses about Scandinavia.
- Students form small groups. Tell students to look at the map and the pictures on pages 62 and 63.
- Have students create a profile of life in Scandinavia based on the information they can gather from the map and pictures. Tell students that it is OK to make guesses, and that they can include any categories they like. (Some possibilities: what the weather is like, what the people are like, what animals live there, etc.)
- If time permits, have groups present their profiles to the class.

1 Study the map. In your notebook, correct the false sentences.
Students correct false information about Scandinavia using a map.

Answers
1. ~~Norway~~ The capital of Sweden is Stockholm.

2 🎧¹⁶ Listen and follow the comic. Then answer the questions.
Students listen and read a dialogue and answer comprehension questions.

Answers
1. They use each other's first names. 2. It's cold. 3. horrible, 4. garbage, 5. Sweden uses Norway's garbage to make energy.

Audio Script
AGNETHA: How are things in Sweden, Lars?
LARS: Good, Agnetha. How's life in Norway?
AGNETHA: Cold! Look, my coffee is frozen!
LARS: But Agnetha, what's that horrible smell? What's in your truck?
AGNETHA: Garbage! I'm taking garbage to Sweden!
LARS: Ugh! Is that for our energy production program?
AGNETHA: Yes. Our countries work together. Your country uses trash to make energy.
LARS: I know. Sweden recycles about 99% of its trash. But we need more to continue producing energy.

Extension
Students make infographics about Scandinavian countries.
- Have students work in small groups.
- Ask them to research some simple facts about one or more Scandinavian countries (population, language, climate, wildlife, currency, economic activity, etc.).
- Have them present their infographics to the rest of the class.

Wrap-up
Students role-play conversations with one of the characters in the dialogue.
- Organize students into pairs have them role-play conversations in which one student interviews the other (playing Lars or Agnetha) about the recycling arrangement that exists between Norway and Sweden.

➡ **(No homework today.)**

> 💭 **Teaching Tip**
> **Connecting Language Learning**
> Make a habit of looking for ways to connect English classes with other parts of the school curriculum (geography, math, history, science, etc.). Try to have non-fiction materials on a wide variety of subjects available for students to read and consult.

Lesson 8 Student's Book pp. 62 and 63

Warm-up
Students review the conversation from the previous lesson.
- With books closed, read aloud quotes from the conversation (excluding names, of course!) and ask students to try to identify which character, Agnetha or Lars, said each line. For example, say, *How are things in Sweden?* (Agnetha)
- Students work in pairs to guess which speaker said each line. The pairs with the most correct guesses win.

3 Choose the best summary.
Students select the best summary of the comic.

Answer
3

> **Extension**
> Students research other environmentally responsible projects.
> - Have students work in small groups.
> - Ask them to find out about projects and initiatives in their own country or in other countries that are environmentally responsible, for example, tree-planting campaigns, urban eco-bikes, paperless offices, etc.

Stop and Think! Value
How does recycling help the planet?
- Organize students into small groups and have them brainstorm ideas about how recycling is good for the planet. (If necessary, write some ideas on the board to get them started.)
- Invite groups to share their ideas with the rest of the class.

Wrap-up
Students prepare a radio news item about recycling.
- Organize students into pairs and have them prepare and present a radio report about Norway and Sweden's recycling program.

➡ **(No homework today.)**

Project

Objective
Students will be able to create a short video to promote a green attitude.

Lesson 9 Student's Book pp. 64 and 65

Warm-up

Students review the names of different substances used to make containers.
- Challenge students to write, in just 30 seconds, a list of substances that are used to make containers. Check answers and write a list on the board (*paper, cardboard, wood, plastic, Styrofoam, rubber, cloth, metal, glass*, etc.)

1 Read the post. Do you agree or disagree. Why?
Students read and respond to a teen's views on garbage disposal.

2 Look at the poster. Answer the questions.
Students study information in a poster and answer comprehension questions.

Answers
1. It shows the decomposition rates of common marine debris items (or common garbage in the ocean). 2. No, the rates are estimated. 3. The bigger the picture, the longer it takes the item to decompose. 4. The paper towel disappears fastest. 5. An aluminum can is worse. 6. The disposable diaper and the plastic bottle share a similar rate of decomposition.

Wrap-up

Students write a response to the post in Activity 1.
- Draw students' attention to the post at the top of the page. Ask them to write a response to Cassie, the writer of the post, expressing their opinion about what people should do with their garbage.
- Tell students to exchange responses and check for accuracy in grammar and spelling.

(No homework today.)

Teaching Tip

Managing Peer Correction
Peer correction can be a very beneficial learning technique: it increases awareness of accuracy in language and spelling. However, it is important that students be respectful of each other's presentations and essays, and focus on giving constructive feedback. Make sure students know what they are checking when revising each other's work, giving examples when necessary.

Lesson 10   Student's Book pp. 64 and 65

Warm-up
Students try to recall information from the poster on these pages.
- With books closed, ask students to try to recall how long specific marine debris items are estimated to take to decompose.
- Then let students open their books to check their answers.

3 Interview 10 classmates and complete the graph.
Students survey classmates about their garbage disposal habits.
- Ask students to look at the graph. Explain that it is designed to show the type of garbage, from a selection of five items, that a person (or a household) produces most in a typical week, for example.
- Tell students that they are going to interview 10 classmates and that they are to record each classmate's answer on the graph. Model a question and answer with a student. Ask *Which of these things does your family throw away?* If the student says *plastic bottles and apple cores*, show students that they should mark one student in the plastic bottle column and one student in the apple core column.
- Have students walk around the classroom, asking and answering and completing their graphs with the numbers of students (up to a total of 10) who throw away each of the five items. Invite various students to share their findings.

4 Make a two-minute video to promote a green attitude. Follow these instructions.
Students create short videos about green attitudes.
- As a whole class, brainstorm ideas about the various formats that students can use: an interview with an expert, a teenager telling a friend about how to recycle, a character (human or otherwise) who shares information, a "before and after" scenario, etc. Discuss how a video can use live actors, or animation, or voiceovers combined with images, etc. Also, point out that the script does not just contain what people say, but it also describes their actions, facial expressions, pauses, etc.
- Organize students into small groups and have them work on their videos.

The Digital Touch
To incorporate digital media in the project, suggest one or more of the following:
- Invite students to explore and use some of the large variety of apps for making videos in the classroom.
- Encourage students to use free video editing software for their videos.
- If possible, allow students to upload their videos to the school's website.

Note that students should have the option to do a task on paper or digitally.

Wrap-up
Students compare videos and vote for their favorites.
- Invite students to vote for their favorite videos. There can be awards in various categories, e.g., best concept, best script, best storyboard, best design, best use of technology, best overall video, etc.

⏵ **Workbook p. 140, Activity 1 (Review)**

Review

Objective
Students will be able to consolidate their understanding of the vocabulary and grammar learned in the unit.

Lesson 11   Student's Book p. 66

> ✔ **Homework Check!**
> Workbook p. 140, Activity 1 (Review)
> **Answers**
> **1 Look at the picture. What is in the fridge?**
> 1. There are some bananas. 2. There aren't any strawberries. 3. There is a lot of cheese. 4. There is a little milk. 5. There are some apples. 6. There is some water. 7. There are some carrots. / There are a few carrots.

Warm-up
Students play Hangman to practice food vocabulary.
- Invite students to play Hangman in two teams, using fruits and vegetables that they have seen in this unit.

1 Complete the puzzle. What is the mystery food?
Students complete a word puzzle with food vocabulary using icons as clues.

Answers
1. lettuce, 2. orange, 3. lime, 4. carrot, 5. potato, 6. onion, 7. apple, 8. strawberry, *mystery food* tomatoes

2 Complete the missing letters in the text.
Students complete the missing letters of words to complete a text about growing fruits and vegetables.

Answers
1. weeds, 2. thumb, 3. seeds, 4. earthworms, 5. snails, 6. caterpillars, 7. fertilizer, 8. water, 9. dig, 10. pick

> **Extension**
> Students research the nutritional properties of fruits and vegetables.
> - Organize students into groups and have them find out about the nutritional properties (minerals, vitamins, carbohydrates, etc.) of various fruits and vegetables.
> - Ask students to report their findings to the rest of the class.

Wrap-up
Students respond to the diary writer.
- Students form pairs and make a list of the problems the writer of the diary mentions in Activity 2.
- Tell pairs to come up with solutions to help the diary writer and note them down.
- Have pairs role-play a conversation about the gardening problems and solutions. Student A will be the writer of the diary, and Student B will be a friend who is trying to help.

➡ **(No homework today.)**

Lesson 12   Student's Book p. 67

Warm-up

Students devise menus for a packed lunch.
- Organize students into small groups and ask them to devise an ideal packed lunch menu. Encourage them to come up with healthy food options. Tell groups to share their ideas with the rest of the class.

3 Read and complete the conversation.

Students complete a conversation with the correct quantifiers.

Answers

1. any, 2. little, 3. much, 4. any, 5. some, 6. few, 7. many

4 Correct the mistakes.

Students correct sentences using quantifiers.

Answers

1. a few Get some lettuce for the salad. 2. many How much spaghetti do you want? 3. few There's only a little rice. 4. many How much butter do you put on your toast? 5. some We don't have any cherries. 6. much How many apples do you have for the pie?

5 Complete these sentences about you.

Students complete sentences with true information about their own lives.

Answers

Answers will vary.

? Big Question

Students are given the opportunity to revisit the Big Question and reflect on it.
- Ask students to turn to the unit opener on page 55 and to look again at the photo, which shows a pair of hands around planet Earth.
- First, ask students to suggest what interpretations they can make of the photo itself. For example, it could represent the idea that the Earth is fragile, that we have to protect the Earth, that the fate of the Earth is in our hands, etc.
- Invite students to share information about things that they do which help to protect the planet.
- As a whole-class activity, discuss other measures that could be taken—by individuals, by communities, by governments—to protect the planet.

★ Scorecard

Hand out (and/or project) a *Scorecard*. Have students fill in their *Scorecards* for this unit.

▶ **Study for the unit test.**

69

5 What does it mean to be happy?

Grammar

Verb be: was, were: My grandmother was three in this picture.

There was/were: There weren't any computers.

Short answers: Yes, I was. No, I wasn't.

Vocabulary

Pastimes: camping, dancing, doing cannonballs, drawing, hanging out with friends, making models, playing board games, popping a wheelie, rollerblading

Reading

Describing a photo

Speaking

Describing a photo

What does it mean to be happy?

In the first lesson, read the unit title aloud and have students look carefully at the unit cover. Encourage them to think about the message in the picture. At the end of the unit, students will discuss the big question: *What does it mean to be happy?*

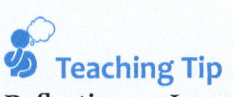

Teaching Tip

Reflecting on Learning

Encourage students to engage in self-reflection at the end of each unit or block of study. Invite them to ask themselves a series of questions to reflect on the learning process, for example, *How well am I doing? What do I find easy / difficult? What do I need to do more of? How can I improve? What resources can I use? How can my teacher help me?*

Vocabulary

Objective

Students will be able to use **pastimes** vocabulary to talk about what they do in their free time.

Lesson 1   Student's Book pp. 70 and 71

Warm-up

Students talk about things that they enjoy doing.
- As a small group activity, invite students to think of and share pastimes that they would most like to be doing at this moment.
- Have groups tell the class everyone's choices and vote on the pastime most students enjoy.

1 🎧¹⁷ **Listen and label the pictures.**

Students label photos with the correct pastimes vocabulary.

Answers

1. popping a wheelie, 2. rollerblading, 3. drawing,
4. playing board games, 5. dancing, 6. camping,
7. making models, 8. doing cannonballs,
9. hanging out with friends

Audio Script

1. This is a picture of me popping a wheelie.
2. You can see me rollerblading in this pic. That was fun!
3. I like drawing a lot. You should see my album of pictures.
4. I love playing board games with my cousin Mike.
5. Here's a picture of me and my friends dancing.
6. Camping is one of my favorite outdoor activities.
7. I love making models.
8. I have a lot of fun doing cannonballs.
9. This is a picture of me hanging out with my friends.

2 Copy the pastimes onto the chart in your notebook. Then complete it.

Students copy and complete a chart sorting pastimes into categories.

Answers

individual drawing, making models, *in groups* hanging out with friends, *done outdoors* camping, rollerblading, *done indoors* playing board games, *very active* dancing, doing cannonballs, *dangerous* popping a wheelie

3 Think Fast! Add two more pastimes to the chart.

Students do a five-minute timed activity: they extend the pastimes chart with more activities.

Answers

Answers will vary.

Wrap-up

Students talk about the activities that they like to do.
- Organize students into small groups and have them exchange information about the activities on these pages that they like to do. Invite students to share their findings with the rest of the class.

▶ **Workbook p. 142, Activities 1 and 2**

Lesson 2   Student's Book p. 71

> ✔ **Homework Check!**
> Workbook p. 142, Activities 1 and 2
> **Answers**
> **1 Unscramble the words to complete the post.**
> 1. rollerblading, 2. board, 3. model, 4. drawing,
> 5. dancing, 6. hanging
> **2 Look and complete the sentences.**
> 1. popping a wheelie, 2. doing cannonballs,
> 3. play board games, 4. drawing, 5. rollerblading,
> 6. dancing

Warm-up
Students discuss preferences for indoor or outdoor activities.
- Organize students into small groups. Elicit one or two pastimes. Then tell them they have two minutes to make a list of as many pastimes as possible.
- Have students share some of their pastimes. Ask students which ones are indoor and which one are outdoor activities.
- In small groups, tell students to say whether they prefer indoor or outdoor pastimes, and why.

4 Complete the sentences.
Students practice pastimes vocabulary and collocations in a sentence completion exercise.
- Draw students' attention to the **Guess What!** box. Read the information aloud and discuss the expression *chilling*. Ask students why they think it is important to have some time to just chill. Ask them what they do when they chill at home.

Answers
1. playing, 2. drawing, 3. rollerblading, 4. hanging out,
5. doing cannonballs, 6. popping a wheelie,
7. making models, 8. camping, 9. listening / dancing

5 Interview your classmates.
Students practice pastimes vocabulary in a speaking activity as they ask their classmates about their pastimes.

Wrap-up
Students interview each other about pastimes.
- Ask students to form pairs with one of the classmates who answered *Yes* to a question in Activity 5. Have the pairs of students interview each other to find out more about the other person's pastime or interest.

➠ **Workbook p. 142, Activity 3**

> 💬 **Teaching Tip**
> **Extending Survey Activities**
> When students are doing *Find someone who…* activities, encourage them to go further than answer with a short, simple *Yes* or *No*, and to offer additional information. For example, in answer to the question, *Do you hang out with your cousins?*, an extended answer would be, for example, *Yes, I do. My cousins and I often play soccer together on weekends.*

Grammar

Objective
Students will be able to use the **past simple of** *be* **(+,–,?)** and *there was / were* to talk about the past.

Lesson 3 — Student's Book pp. 72 and 73

> ✔ Homework Check!
> Workbook page 142, Activity 3
> **Answers**
> **3 Match the pieces to make sentences.**
> 1. d, 2. f, 3. a, 4. b, 5. e

Warm-up

Students exchange information about their grandparents.
- Organize students into small groups and have them share information about their grandparents, in particular physical descriptions (e.g., tall, short, long hair) and personalities (e.g., happy, serious), etc. Invite students to share information with the rest of the class.

74

1 🎧18 Listen and complete the sentences.
Students listen to a text describing photos and complete sentences with words from the audio.

Answers

1. birthday, 2. eighth, 3. serious, 4. fast, 5. house

Audio Script
My grandmother was three in this picture. She wasn't sad at her birthday party. She was very happy. Here, my grandma and her friends were in eighth grade. They weren't in high school yet. In this picture, my grandfather wasn't angry. He was just serious. This was my grandfather's typewriter. It wasn't fast like a computer. Look at this! I was two in this picture. We were at my grandmother's house in LA.

2 Read the sentences above and number the pictures.
Students number the photos in order to match the sequence the photos are discussed in the audio.

Answers

top to bottom 3, 4, 1, 5, 2

3 Look at the pictures and circle the correct options.
Students complete sentences with the correct form of the past simple of *be*.
- Draw students' attention to the **Past of** *be* box. Remind students that, unlike the present simple, which has three forms (*am, are, is*), the past simple has only two forms (*was, were*).

Answers

1. was, 2. was, 3. wasn't, 4. weren't

Extension
Students talk about their grandparents.
- Invite students to prepare short, illustrated presentations about the lives of their grandparents. If they are able to obtain permission from their family members, encourage them to include photos and authentic documents to illustrate the lives of their grandparents.

Wrap-up

Students write sentences using the past simple of *be*.
- Ask students to write eight sentences about their grandparents (or other family members) when they were younger: two sentences with *was*, two sentences with *wasn't*, two sentences with *were* and two sentences with *weren't*.

➡ **Workbook p. 143, Activities 1 and 2**

Lesson 4
Student's Book pp. 72 and 73

> ✔ **Homework Check!**
> Workbook p. 143, Activities 1 and 2
> **Answers**
> **1 Write the sentences in past.**
> 1. I was cold in the morning. 2. We were late for the math exam. 3. They were in LA for the weekend. 4. It was a good book. 5. Your answer was right. 6. She was tired after gym class.
> **2 In your notebook, change the sentences in Activity 1 to negative.**
> 1. I wasn't cold in the morning. 2. We weren't late for the math exam. 3. They weren't in LA for the weekend. 4. It wasn't a good book. 5. Your answer wasn't right. 6. She wasn't tired after gym class.

Warm-up
Students listen and respond to sentences using the past simple form of *be*.
- With books closed, read aloud a series of sentences using *was*, *wasn't*, *were* and *weren't*. Say, for example, *Your parents weren't at home yesterday evening.* or *Your mother was at work yesterday morning.* Have students simply raise their hands whenever they hear a sentence that is true for them and their families.

4 Look at the photo. Decide if the sentences are *T* (True) or *F* (False).
Students mark sentences as true or false based on a photo.

Answers
1. T, 2. F (There wasn't a TV in the classroom.), 3. F (There weren't cell phones.), 4. T

5 Think Fast! What was there in your classroom in primary school?
Students do a one-minute timed challenge: they talk about their primary school classrooms.

Answers
Answers will vary.

6 Use *was* or *were* to complete the questions. Then answer the questions.
Students complete and answer questions using the correct past simple forms of *be*.

1. were, 2. was, 3. Were, 4. Was
Answers will vary.

Wrap-up
Students play a memory game to practice *There was*, *There were*, etc.
- Ask two students to leave the room. While they are gone, remove certain items from so that, for example, there are no longer any marker pens for the board, or there is no longer a chair for the teacher. Have the students come back into the room and have them try to identify what has changed, for example, *There was a chair here.*

▶ **Workbook pp. 143 and 144, Activities 3–5**

🐝 Teaching Tip
Making Connections
The topic of this lesson, in which students talk about people's lives in the past and what there was (or wasn't) in the past, lends itself to cross-curricular work with the history department of your school. Look for ways to enrich students' learning of English by finding links with other areas of the school curriculum: science, art, social sciences, music, etc.

Reading & Writing

Objectives
Students will be able to identify the order of events. They will also be able to describe events in an organized, coherent way.

Lesson 5   Student's Book pp. 74 and 75

✔ **Homework Check!**
Workbook pp. 143 and 144, Activities 3–5
Answers
3 Complete and answer the questions.
1. Were, weren't, 2. Was, wasn't, 3. Were, were, 4. Were, weren't, 5. Was, was, 6. Was, was
4 Circle and correct one mistake in each sentence.
1. ~~Was~~ Were we at your party last week?
2. ~~weren't~~ My brother wasn't at his music lesson.
3. ~~wasn't~~ There weren't any people at the bus stop yesterday. 4. ~~was~~ Jim and Emmy were in the living room. 5. ~~were~~ There was a great program on TV last night.
5 Look and complete the sentences with *there was / wasn't* **or** *there were / weren't*.
1. There were, 2. there weren't, 3. there wasn't, 4. There wasn't, 5. There was, 6. There were, 7. There were, 8. there wasn't, 9. there wasn't

Warm-up
Students talk about amusement parks.
- As a small-group activity, and with books closed, invite students to share information about amusement parks that they have visited or that they have heard of in their own country or in other countries. Try to elicit the expression *roller coaster*.

1 Read the e-mail and number the pictures.
Students identify the order of events in a text and number corresponding pictures.
Answers
top to bottom 3, 1, 2

2 Read the e-mail again and label the people.
Students scan the same text for more detailed information to identify the people in the photos.
Answers
top to bottom Wendy, Melanie, Pedro, Arturo, Sean, Tania

Extension
Students talk about what there is in an amusement park.
- Organize students into small groups and ask them to discuss what there is in an amusement park. Have them draw up lists and then present their ideas to the rest of the class using *There is* and *There are*.

Wrap-up
Students role-play a conversation based on an e-mail.
- Organize students into pairs and have them role-play a conversation between Tania (the girl who wrote the e-mail) and a friend in which she tells of a trip to an amusement park.

➡ **Workbook p. 145, Activity 1**

Lesson 6 Student's Book pp. 74 and 75

> ✔ **Homework Check!**
> Workbook p. 145, Activity 1
>
> **Answers**
> **1 Read the article and label the people in the pictures.**
> 1. Hugh, 2. Luke, 3. Tom, 4. Jess, 5. Louise,
> 6. Jeremy, 7. Dana, 8. Carrie, 9. George

Warm-up
Students review prepositions of place.
- Set a time limit of, say, one minute and ask students to write a list of as many prepositions of place (*in, on, under, next to*, etc.) as they can think of. Check answers and write examples on the board.

3 Look at the highlighted phrases in the e-mail and complete the expressions below.
Students complete phrases with prepositions of place from the text.

Answers
1. an amusement park, 2. front, 3. left, 4. me,
5. Pedro, 6. middle, 7. back

4 Choose a photo and describe it to your partner. Your partner points at the correct picture.
Students describe photos orally for a partner to identify.
- Draw students' attention to the ***Be Strategic!*** box. Read the information aloud and discuss the importance of using adjectives and expressions such as prepositions of place for describing people and places.

Stop and Think! Critical Thinking
Are friends important to make you happy?
- Organize students into small groups and have them discuss the question. (If necessary, write some ideas on the board to get them started.)
- Invite groups to share their ideas with the rest of the class.

Wrap-up
Students play a game using prepositions of place.
- Organize students into teams. Have them write five sentences about the location or position of five mystery objects or pieces of furniture in their classroom.
- Then, a student from one team reads aloud a sentence, for example, *This object is behind the teacher's table.* Members of another team try to identify the mystery object.

▶ **Workbook p. 145, Activity 2**

Preparing for the Next Lesson
Ask students to watch an introduction to the Bedouin: goo.gl/G6cuQG.

Culture

Objectives
Students will be able to talk about the Arabian Peninsula and the culture of the Bedouin. They will also develop awareness of cultural diversity.

Lesson 7 — Student's Book pp. 76 and 77

> ✔ **Homework Check!**
> Workbook page 145, Activity 2
> **Answers**
> **2 Read the article again and circle T (True) or F (False).**
> 1. F, 2. T, 3. F (People roll around in the balls like hamsters do.), 4. F (The competition was for skating, including skateboarding.), 5. F (The winner was Tom.), 6. F (They are eating marshmallows, a type of candy.)

Warm-up
Students answer quick quiz questions about the Arabian Peninsula.
- With books closed, ask students a series of questions about the Arabian Peninsula, using the text on this page as the source of information. The questions can be multiple-choice, for example, *How many countries make up the Arabian Peninsula: five, seven, or nine?* (Seven)

1 Read the introduction of the article and complete the mind map.
Students read a text and organize the information in a mind map.

Answers
middle Saudi Arabia, *clockwise* Arabic, Friday and Saturday, Bedouin, over 40°C, oil, Riyadh

2 Read the article on page 77 and mark (✓) the topics mentioned.
Students skim a text and identify the main topics.

Answers
animals, family, hospitality

> **Extension**
> Students make mind maps about their countries.
> - Invite students to create a mind map about the region of the world where they live and their own country, using the mind map on this page as a model. Have them include information about language, temperatures, capital city, etc.
> - Ask students to share their mind maps with the rest of the class.

Wrap-up
Students write an introductory paragraph about their country in pairs.
- Tell pairs to write an introduction for an article about their country, using the text on this page as a model.
- Invite students to share their work with the rest of the class.

➡ **(No homework today.)**

Lesson 8 Student's Book pp. 76 and 77

Warm-up
Students discuss what it would be like to live in a desert.
- As a small-group activity, discuss what students think it would be like to live in the deserts of Arabia, like the Bedouin.

3 Read again and answer the questions in your notebook.
Students scan a text and answer comprehension questions.

Answers
1. No. They live in tents and travel from place to place. 2. The family is where children learn the values of the community. 3. Camels provide transportation, milk, food and clothing. 4. Because they provide transportation and are very important to the Bedouin way of life. 5. Bedouins feel other people in the desert should be treated with respect and kindness.

Stop and Think! Value
How does taking care of others make you happy?
- Organize students into small groups and have them discuss the question. (If necessary, write some ideas on the board to get them started.)
- Invite groups to share their ideas with the rest of the class.

Wrap-up
Students discuss their reactions to what they have read.
- Organize students into small groups and ask them to compare and discuss their reactions to what they read in the article about the Bedouin.
- As a whole-class discussion, have students exchange ideas and opinions. Encourage them to compare and contrast the culture of the Bedouin with that of their own society.

➡ (No homework today.)

💬 Teaching Tip
Encouraging Comparison of Cultures
Always encourage students to compare and contrast societies and cultures of other countries with their own, not in a judgmental way, looking for ways in which one culture is superior or inferior to another, but as a way to enhance their understanding and appreciation of the diversity of the world's cultures.

Project

Objective
Students will be able to design and conduct a survey.

Lesson 9
Student's Book pp. 78 and 79

Warm-up
Students discuss different types of surveys and how the information from surveys is used.
- In small groups, tell students to discuss the types of survey that they are familiar with, for example, surveys in teenage magazines, online surveys, surveys conducted in the street, telephone surveys, etc.
- Also, ask students to speculate about how the people who collect information in surveys might be able to use it.

1 Read the quotes. Circle the one you like best. What's the most popular one in the class?
Students discuss and vote on quotes on the subject of happiness.

2 Think Fast! List five things that make you happy.
Students do a one-minute timed challenge: they brainstorm and make a list of things that make them happy.

Answers
Answers will vary.

3 Read the survey report on the next page and circle T (True) or F (False).
Students read a survey report and mark statements about the report as true or false.

Answers
1. F (The size of the sample was 24 students.), 2. T, 3. F (Best friends are the second preferred choice.), 4. F (Most students like having their own bedroom.), 5. F (Only a small number of students think money makes them happy.), 6. T

Wrap-up
Students compare and discuss their reactions to the information in the report.
- Organize students into small groups and ask them to compare and discuss their reactions to what they read in the report.
- As a whole-class discussion, have students exchange comments and observations.

Lesson 10 — Student's Book pp. 78 and 79

Warm-up
Students review simple fractions as represented in pie charts.
- Draw a series of circles on the board and on each one mark one of the following fractions, as in a pie chart: one fourth (one quarter), one third, one half, two thirds, three quarters. Elicit the correct expression for the proportion marked on each circle.

4 In your notebook, change the highlighted fractions in the survey to percentages.

Students convert fractions written as words into percentage values.

Answers
50%, 25%, 66.6%, 75%, 33.3%

5 Design a survey report on what makes teenagers happy. Follow these instructions.

Students create survey reports about what makes teenagers happy.
- Read aloud the instructions and make sure that students understand the steps that they are to follow.
- Organize students into small groups and have them work on their surveys. Then, once they have gathered their data, have them prepare pie charts to show their results and written reports to summarize their findings.

The Digital Touch
To incorporate digital media in the project, suggest one or more of the following:
- Encourage students to use free online survey and questionnaire tools.
- Have students present their findings from their surveys using PowerPoint or similar slide show presentation programs like Google Slides.
- If possible, allow students to upload their work to the school's website.

Note that students should have the option to do a task on paper or digitally.

Wrap-up
Students compare surveys and reports and vote for their favorites.
- Invite students to vote for their favorite presentations of their classmates' surveys. There can be awards in various categories, e.g., best design, best use of graphics, best use of technology, best overall presentation, etc.

➡ **Workbook p. 144, Activity 1 (Review)**

Teaching Tip
Working in Teams
When doing project work in groups, stress to students the importance of the idea that students "sink or swim" together. This can be achieved by making part of each student's grade dependent on the performance of the rest of the team. Group members must believe that each person's efforts benefit not only him- or herself, but all group members as well.

Review

Objective
Students will be able to consolidate their understanding of the vocabulary and grammar learned in the unit.

Lesson 11 Student's Book p. 80

> ✔ **Homework Check!**
> Workbook page 144, Activity 1 (Review)
> **Answers**
> **1 Look at the picture and write sentences.**
> 1. There was a birthday party. 2. There was cake.
> 3. There were gifts. 4. There was rock music.
> 5. There was soda.

Warm-up
Students review pastimes vocabulary playing a game.
- Review pastimes vocabulary from page 70 (drawing, playing board games, rollerblading, etc.) by playing Hangman.

1 Follow and write the activities.
Students label photos of pastimes.

Answers
top to bottom playing board games, camping, making models, doing cannonballs, rollerblading, popping a wheelie

2 Cross out the options that don't belong.
Students cross out the words or phrases that don't make sense in each sentence.

Answers
1. play board games, 2. drawing, 3. do cannonballs, 4. hanging out, 5. camping, 6. making models, 7. popping a wheelie, 8. dancing

3 Circle the correct options.
Students complete sentences with the correct forms of the past simple of *be*.

Answers
1. was, 2. were, 3. weren't, 4. Were, 5. were, 6. wasn't, 7. wasn't, 8. weren't

> **Extension**
> Students make vocabulary posters.
> - Invite students to design and create illustrated vocabulary posters showing a variety of pastimes.
> - Alternatively, ask students to create advertisements for a camp or a summer course where teenagers can participate in a variety of activities, both indoor and outdoor.
> - Display students' work around the classroom.

Wrap-up
Students practice the past simple of *be* by playing a guessing game.
- Divide the class into two teams. In silence, a player from one team chooses a place where they were yesterday (at the mall, at school, etc.), who they were with (with friends, alone, etc.) and how they were feeling (happy, nervous, etc.). Players from the other team ask up to a maximum of ten yes/no questions to try to discover all the correct information, for example,
Q: *Were you with your family?*
A: *Yes, I was. / No, I wasn't.*

➡ **(No homework today.)**

Lesson 12   Student's Book p. 81

Warm-up

Students talk briefly about where they were and who they were with at different times yesterday.
- Write a series of times on the board, for example, 8:00 a.m., 10:30 a.m., 12:30 p.m., 4:00 p.m., 8:30 p.m., 11:00 p.m. and have students work in pairs exchanging information about where they were and who they were with at these times yesterday.
- Have students report to the class what their partners told them.

4 Complete the conversation with *was* or *were* in the correct form.

Students complete a conversation with the correct forms of the past simple of *be*.

Answers

1. was, 2. were, 3. was, 4. wasn't, 5. Were, 6. weren't, 7. were, 8. Was, 9. was, 10. was, 11. wasn't, 12. were, 13. was, 14. were

5 Complete the description with the words below.

Students describe locations in a photo in a completion exercise.

Answers

1. top, 2. left, 3. back, 4. right, 5. middle

6 Complete these sentences so they are true for you.

Students complete sentences about their pastimes.

Answers

Answers will vary.

? Big Question

Students are given the opportunity to revisit the Big Question and reflect on it.
- Ask students to turn to the unit opener on page 69 and to look again at the collage of photos, which shows a variety of people doing activities that make them happy.
- First, ask students to offer ideas about specific photos and to say what they think the people are doing and why it makes them happy.
- Discuss the way shared activities (with family, friends, teammates, colleagues, etc.) often produce feelings of happiness and ask students to say why they think this is. Also, talk about how personal achievements (winning a race, completing a project, passing an exam, etc.) bring satisfaction and happiness.

★ Scorecard

Hand out (and/or project) a *Scorecard*. Have students fill in their *Scorecards* for this unit.

➡ **Study for the unit test.**

6 Where do bright ideas come from?

Grammar
Past simple: Humans wore animal skins. They didn't wear modern clothes. Did they discover fire recently?

Vocabulary
The Scientific Method: analyze data, ask a question, do an experiment, do research, draw conclusions, write a hypothesis

Adjectives and Prepositions: busy with, excited about, good at, interested in, nervous about, worried about

Listening
Anticipating information

Writing
Researching and writing a biography

Where do bright ideas come from?

In the first lesson, read the unit title aloud and have students look carefully at the unit cover. Encourage them to think about the message in the picture. At the end of the unit, students will discuss the big question: *Where do bright ideas come from?*

Teaching Tip
Using Your Voice

As much as possible, use your normal, natural voice. If you talk at an above-normal volume, sooner or later you will lose your voice! If you raise the level of your voice, students will tend to do the same and the noise level will escalate. Also, try to differentiate your tone. If you are asking students to put away their notebooks and get into their groups, use a more declarative, matter-of-fact tone. If you are asking students about their favorite movies or what they think of Chinese food, use an inviting, conversational tone.

Vocabulary

Objective
Students will be able to use **scientific method** and **adjectives and prepositions** vocabulary to talk about science.

Lesson 1   Student's Book pp. 84 and 85

Warm-up
Students talk the last time they had a bright idea.
- Write the phrase *a bright idea* on the board and ask students to say what they think it means. Elicit the idea that a bright idea is a good idea, an original idea that perhaps nobody has had before. Talk about how many inventions and innovations start as bright ideas.
- In small groups, invite students to talk about the last time they had a bright idea, what gave them the idea, and how they felt when they had the idea.

1 Decode the missing verbs. (43 = S, 15 = E, etc.)
Students decipher a number / letter code.
- Tell students to look at the six numbered boxes that stretch across these two pages and that describe a scientific process. Elicit or point out that the verb in each caption is written in a number code. Tell students that 43 = S and that 15 = E and write the alphabet and the corresponding numbers on the board.

Answers
1. ask, 2. do, 3. write, 4. do, 5. analyze, 6. draw

2 Match the steps of the scientific method above to their explanation.
Students match the steps of the scientific method with the steps in an explanation of how Kelly Reese developed her invention.

Answers
1. d, 2. c, 3. a, 4. b, 5. e, 6. f

3 Identify and number the events according to the scientific method.
Students number a series of steps according to the scientific method.

Answers
top to bottom 1, 6, 4, 5, 3, 2

Stop and Think! Critical Thinking
When do you feel inspired to solve a problem?
- Organize students into small groups and have them discuss the question. (If necessary, write some ideas on the board to get them started.)
- Invite groups to share their ideas with the rest of the class.

Wrap-up
Students discuss their reactions to the two scientific projects covered in these pages in small groups.
- Review the two scientific projects—Kelly's invention and the experiment with the tomatoes. Then ask students to work in small groups discussing their reactions to the two projects. Ask some questions to get students started. Ask, for example, *Which of the two projects do you find more interesting? Which project is more useful?*
- Have groups share their observations and comments with the rest of the class.

➡ **Workbook p. 146, Activity 1**

Teaching Tip
Using Real-Life Examples
Look for opportunities to relate coursebook content with the real world to make it more meaningful and memorable. For example, tell students about a real-life young inventor who has been in the news recently, or share information about some agricultural innovations that have been tested in the students' country recently.

Lesson 2   Student's Book p. 85

> ✔ **Homework Check!**
> Workbook p. 146, Activity 1
>
> **Answers**
> **1 Unscramble the sentences and decode the message.**
> *top to bottom* ask a question, do research, write a hypothesis, analyze data, draw conclusions, The scientific method is an organized way to solve problems.

Warm-up

Students review the steps of the scientific method.

- Form groups of six students. Give each person in a group a slip of paper with one of the steps of the scientific method written on it: *analyze data, ask a question, do an experiment, do research, draw conclusions, write a hypothesis*. (Make sure each group has a complete set of steps.)
- Have groups read the slips of paper and quickly stand in a line, according to the correct order of the scientific method.

Answers
first person ask a question, *second* do research, *third* write a hypothesis, *fourth* do an experiment, *fifth* analyze data, *sixth* draw conclusions

4 Complete the mind map with the highlighted expressions in Activity 1.

Students complete a mind map with adjective and preposition collocations.

Answers
left to right, top to bottom about – worried, nervous, excited, *good* – at, interested – in, busy – *with*

5 Answer the questions.

Students answer questions with information that is true for them.

Answers
Answers will vary.

> ### Extension
> Students talk about interests, talents and feelings.
> - Organize students into pairs and have them exchange information about their interests, their abilities and how they feel about certain things. To get them started, write a few sample questions on the board, for example, *What singer or band are you excited about these days? What are you sometimes worried about? What school assignments are you busy with at the moment?*

Wrap-up

Students interview each other.

- With their notebooks closed, tell students to interview each other in pairs using the questions in Activity 5.
- Encourage students to expand on their answers.

▶ Workbook p. 146, Activities 2 and 3

Grammar

Objective
Students will be able to use **past simple** to talk about people's achievements.

Lesson 3 — Student's Book pp. 86 and 87

> ✔ **Homework Check!**
> Workbook p. 146, Activities 2 and 3
>
> **Answers**
> **2 Number the sentences according to the scientific method.**
> *top to bottom* 1, 4, 6, 5, 2, 3
> **3 Write the missing words.**
> 1. busy with, 2. at, 3. excited about, 4. in,
> 5. worried

Warm-up
Students review past simple verb forms.
- Write on the board the following sentences from the texts about Kelly, leaving spaces for the past simple verbs: *Kelly Reese _____ (get) inspiration from her grandmother. Kelly _____ (be) worried about her grandma. The results of the experiment _____ (be) good! The electronic rug _____ (work).*
- Have students come to the board and complete each space with the correct past simple form.

Answers
got, was, were, worked

1 🎧¹⁹ **Listen and complete the sentences.**
Students listen and complete past simple sentences with verbs from the audio.

Audio Script
1. Humans didn't discover fire recently. They discovered it about one million years ago. Discovered. D-I-S-C-O-V-E-R-E-D
2. Early people painted about everyday life. They didn't paint elaborate pictures. Painted. P-A-I-N-T-E-D
3. Humans wore animal skins. They didn't wear modern clothes. Wore. W-O-R-E
4. Early people had dogs. They didn't have exotic pets. Had. H-A-D
5. Our ancestors didn't invent sophisticated machines, but they invented the wheel. Invented. I-N-V-E-N-T-E-D
6. People didn't write their first words on paper. They wrote them on clay tablets. Wrote. W-R-O-T-E

2 Complete the chart using the verbs in the comic.
Students complete a verb chart about the past simple using verbs from Activity 1.
- Draw students' attention the ***Guess What!*** box. Read the information aloud and discuss how the great majority of verbs in English are regular in the past simple. However, point out also that many of the most common, frequently used verbs in English are irregular.

Answers
Regular Verbs paint – painted, invent – invented
Irregular Verbs have – had, write – wrote

3 Complete the sentences with verbs in the past simple.
Students complete sentences with verbs in the past simple.

Answers
1. wrote, 2. painted, 3. had, 4. wore,
5. discovered, 6. invented

4 In your notebook, write the sentences above in negative form.
Students convert affirmative past simple sentences into negative ones.
- Draw students' attention to the **Past Simple – Auxiliary** box. Read the information aloud and elicit a few examples.

Answers
1. I didn't write an e-mail to my best friend.
2. My brother didn't paint the front of the house last week. 3. We didn't have English class yesterday. 4. We didn't wear our favorite T-shirts. 5. The scientist didn't discover a new species of insect. 6. They didn't invent a new dance.

Wrap-up
Students find sentences and convert them from affirmative to negative or vice versa.
- Have students work in pairs finding affirmative and negative sentences in the past simple on pages 86 and 87. Tell pairs to make the affirmative sentences negative and vice versa.
- Ask pairs what happened to the story in the comic when they reversed the sentences.

➡ **Workbook p. 147, Activities 1 and 2**

Lesson 4 Student's Book p. 87

> ✔ Homework Check!
> Workbook p. 147, Activities 1 and 2
> Answers
> **1 Complete the story using the past simple.**
> 1. saw, 2. ran, 3. walked, 4. felt, 5. discovered, 6. decided, 7. woke
> **2 Complete the chart using the verbs in Activity 1.**
> *Regular* walked, discovered, decided
> *Irregular* saw, ran, felt, woke

Warm-up
Students complete a table with affirmative and negative forms of past simple verbs.
- Draw on the board a simple table with two columns, *Affirmative* on the left-hand side and *Negative* on the right. Partially complete the columns with a selection of familiar and not so familiar verbs and tell students to complete the table in small groups.

5 Match the sentences and questions.
Students match statements in the past simple with yes/no questions.

Answers

1. e, 2. c, 3. b, 4. d, 5. a

6 Change the sentences to affirmative (+), negative (−) or interrogative (?). Use the verb list on page 168.
Students practice the forms of the past simple by transforming sentences.

Answers

1. Sheila didn't go to drama class this morning.
2. You found your keys. 3. Did early people have birds as pets? 4. Your mom cooked something delicious yesterday. 5. Did they like the new sci-fi movie? 6. My father didn't work late last night.

Extension
Students practice affirmative and negative statements in the past simple in a game.
- Play this game as a whole class. One student begins to tell in detail all the things that they did since they woke up in the morning. At any time, another student can interrupt and say, *No, you didn't.* at which point the first speaker has to accept the interruption, make a small correction, and then continue. For example, a "story" might go something like this:
A: This morning, I woke up at seven o'clock. I went downstairs…
B: No, you didn't.
A: Oh, yes. I went to the bathroom. Then I went downstairs. I had my breakfast…
B: No, you didn't. etc. etc.

Wrap-up
Students identify affirmative, negative and question forms of the past simple.
- In quick succession, read aloud a random mixture of past simple sentences: some affirmative, some negative, and some yes/no questions. Have students listen and write +, −, or ? according to the type of sentence.

➡ **Workbook pp. 147 and 148, Activities 3–5**

Teaching Tip
Memorizing Irregular Verb Forms
Be aware that students will most likely need a lot of time to really memorize all the irregular past simple forms that they need, given that so many of the most frequently used verbs are irregular in the simple past. Therefore, it is important to offer lots of repetition, lots of practice and lots of opportunities for students to use past simple verbs in real or realistic contexts. Also, if students feel discouraged about the challenge of memorizing lists of irregular verbs, reassure them that this is normal for all learners.

Listening & Writing

Objectives
Students will be able to identify specific information in a listening. They will also be able to research and write a biography.

Lesson 5 — Student's Book p. 88

✔ **Homework Check!**
Workbook pp. 147 and 148, Activities 3–5

Answers
3 Find and write eleven irregular verbs in the past simple.

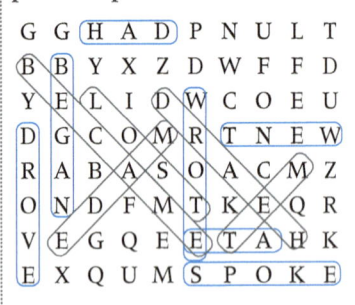

```
G G H A D P N U L T
B B Y X Z D W F F D
Y E L I D W C O E U
D G C O M R T N E W
R A B A S O A C M Z
O N D F M T K E Q R
V E G Q E E T A H K
E X Q U M S P O K E
```

1. had, 2. began, 3. drove, 4. spoke, 5. wrote, 5. became, 6. went, 7. ate, 8. heard, 9. made, 10. met, 11. lost

4 Cross out the mistakes and then correct them.
1. ~~smileed~~ smiled, 2. ~~cryed~~ cried, 3. ~~tiped~~ tipped, 4. ~~eraseed~~ erased, 5. ~~joged~~ jogged, 6. ~~tryed~~ tried

5 Complete the conversation with the past simple of the verbs in parentheses.
1. invented, 2. used, 3. did it feel, 4. felt, 5. looked, 6. went, 7. Did you fall, 8. didn't fall, 9. Did the police see, 10. asked, 11. spoke

Warm-up

Students discuss famous inventors and innovators from the past.
- Organize students into small groups and set a stopwatch for two minutes.
- Tell groups to race to brainstorm the names of inventors from history and their key achievements. The group that lists the most inventors by the end of two minutes wins. If necessary, write a list on the board to get students started: *Alexander Graham Bell – telephone, Thomas Edison – light bulb, Johannes Gutenberg – printing press.*

1 Complete the mind map with five words related to Steve Jobs.
Students brainstorm equipment related to Steve Jobs, using the photos on the page as clues.

Answers
Answers will vary.

2 🎧²⁰ Listen to a podcast. Mark (✓) your words from Activity 1 if you hear them.
Students listen and check their ideas from Activity 1.
- Draw students' attention to the **Be Strategic!** box. Read the information aloud and discuss the usefulness of predicting key words, names, dates, etc. before listening to a broadcast or a video.

Answers
Answers will vary.

Extension
Students create surveys about the importance of technology in their lives.
- Organize students into small groups and have them create survey questionnaires about the technology that people use, the technology that is most important in their lives, etc.
- Invite students to conduct surveys and to report their findings back to the class.

Wrap-up

Students review facts about the life and work of Steve Jobs by role-playing an interview.
- Students form pairs. Tell students to imagine that they could have interviewed Steve Jobs before he died.
- Have one student play the interviewer and another play Jobs. Give interviewers a couple of minutes to develop their questions.
- Encourage students to focus their interviews on the topic of how Jobs came up with his ideas.

➡ **Workbook p. 149, Activity 1**

Lesson 6 Student's Book pp. 88 and 89

> ✔ **Homework Check!**
> Workbook p. 149, Activity 1
> **Answers**
> **1 Read the text and complete the fact file on Robert Louis Stevenson.**
> *top to bottom* 1850, Scotland; engineering at the University of Edinburgh; *Treasure Island, Strange Case of Doctor Jekyll and Mister Hyde*; Long John Silver, Dr. Jekyll; 1894, Samoa

Warm-up

Students check and recall facts from the life and work of Steve Jobs.

- Read aloud a few items from the audio script, some true and some false. Say, for example, *Jobs and Wozniak started their own company in 1984 (false – 1977)*. Have students identify and correct the false statements.

3 🎧²⁰ **Listen again. Complete the biography of Steve Jobs on page 89.**

Students listen and complete a biography with dates.

Answers

1. 1955, 2. 1971, 3. 1976, 4. 1977, 5. 1985,
6. 1986, 7. 1996, 8. 2001, 9. 2003, 10. 2007,
11. 2010, 12. 2011

Audio Script

INTERVIEWER: Today Julio will talk about the life of Steve Jobs. Julio, tell us, when was Steve Jobs born?
JULIO: He was born in San Francisco on February 24th, 1955. He grew up in Silicon Valley and went to university at Reed College, but he dropped out after a year.
I: Now, tell us about Steve Jobs and Steve Wozniak. How did they meet?
J: Well, In 1971 Steve Jobs had a summer job at Hewlett Packard, a company that makes computers and printers. He met Steve Wozniak there. In 1976, Wozniak invented his first computer. Then two years later, in 1977, Steve Jobs and Steve Wozniak started their own company, Apple. He worked there until 1985, when he left. But he joined Pixar, the movie studio in 1986. The movie studio is famous for movies like *Toy Story* and *Finding Nemo*. Ten years later, in 1996, he returned to Apple.
I: And that's when Apple produced the iPod, right?
J: That's right. Apple produced the iPod mp3 player in 2001. [pause] Then tragedy. Jobs discovered he had cancer in 2003. This was obviously terrible news, but he continued working and several years later, Apple produced the iPhone in 2007.
I: What about the iPad?
J: Apple invented it in 2010. Unfortunately, Jobs died the next year, on October 5th, 2011, at 56. He was one of the greatest minds of this century.

4 Write a biography. Use the text in Activity 3 as a guide. Follow the instructions below.

Students write a biography guided by instructions and the model in Activity 3.

Stop and Think! Critical Thinking

What type of personality is needed to produce good ideas?

- Organize students into small groups and have them discuss the people they read about in the unit so far who had good ideas.

- Then ask *Do the people have anything in common? What do you think their personalities were like?*

- Invite groups to share their ideas about the type of personality needed to produce good ideas with the rest of the class.

Wrap-up

Students share their biographies from Activity 4.

- In small groups, have students read their biographies. Students listening take notes and later ask questions.

▶ **Workbook p. 149, Activities 2 (Reading) and 1 (Writing)**

Preparing for the Next Lesson

Ask students to consult an introduction to Chile: goo.gl/IPTHKh and to watch a video about the Alma telescopes: goo.gl/8A2u0M.

Culture

Objective
Students will be able to talk about Chile, the Atacama Desert and the Alma telescopes project. They will also develop awareness of technological innovation.

Lesson 7 — Student's Book pp. 90 and 91

✔ **Homework Check!**
Workbook p. 149, Activities 2 (Reading) and 1 (Writing)

Answers
2 Read the text again and circle *T* (True) or *F* (False).
1. F (Stevenson wrote *Treasure Island* in 1881-1882.), 2. T, 3. F (Stevenson studied engineering at university.), 4. T, 5. T, 6. F (Stevenson died at the age of 44.)
1 Write a one-paragraph biography of an author you like in your notebook. Use these notes to help you.
Answers will vary.

Warm-up (p. 92)
Students test their knowledge of the geography of South America.
- As a whole-class activity, conduct a quick-fire quiz about South America. Ask about capital cities, languages, cultural sites, customs, food, etc.

1 Read and label the map using the highlighted names in the text.
Students read a text and find information in the text to label a map.

Answers
top to bottom Andes Mountains, Atacama Desert, Santiago, Cape Horn

2 🎧²¹ Look at the photos. Then listen and answer the questions.
Students listen to an interview and answer comprehension questions.

Answers
1. The Atacama Desert. 2. Yes, there are telescopes. 3. To study the stars.

Audio Script
Interviewer: Renata, we're in the Atacama Desert in Chile. Tell us about it.
Renata: Well, the climate here is very dry. The Atacama Desert is in the north of Chile. The desert is 1,000 square kilometers and nobody lives here.
I: And the Atacama Desert is the home of Alma, an international project to study the stars. Renata, why the Atacama Desert?
R: Because it's perfect for astronomy. It's very dry, so there aren't many clouds in the sky. The altitude is perfect. Also there is very little light pollution.
I: Light pollution?
R: Cities and towns generate a lot of light and it's impossible to see the stars. That's not a problem here.
I: How many telescopes do you have?
R: We have ten enormous and very powerful telescopes here.
I: And this is an international project?
R: Yes. We need the knowledge of experts from all around the world. Chile works with scientists from countries in Asia, Europe, as well as the U.S. and Canada. Alma's work in Chile is an example of global collaboration. People can do amazing things when they work together.

3 🎧²¹ Listen again and correct the false information in each sentence.
Students listen closely and correct false information in statements about the audio.

Answers
1. ~~10~~ The desert is 1,000 square kilometers. 2. ~~fauna~~ Alma is an international project to study the stars. 3. ~~birds~~ It's very dry, so there aren't many clouds in the sky. 4. ~~tiny~~ We have ten enormous and very powerful telescopes here. 5. ~~money~~ We need the knowledge of experts from all around the world. 6. ~~national~~ Alma's work in Chile is an example of global collaboration.

Wrap-up
Students create information posters about the Alma telescopes.
- Have students work in groups creating information posters about the Alma telescopes. Display students' work around the classroom.

➡ **(No homework today.)**

Lesson 8   Student's Book pp. 90 and 91

Warm-up

Students discuss different types of puzzles.
- As a whole-class activity, elicit the names of different types of puzzle: crossword puzzles, logic puzzles, wordsearch puzzles, math puzzles, etc.
- Invite students to say what kinds of puzzles they enjoy solving and why.

◄ **Think Fast! Try to solve the puzzle on your own.**
Students do a one-minute timed challenge: they try to solve a logic puzzle working alone.
- Ask students to look at the puzzle. Read aloud the instructions and ask students to copy the picture of the puzzle in their books. If possible, provide students with used matches, toothpicks or similar so that they can make the figure on their desks.

5 Do the puzzle above in small groups. Check your answer on page 96. Then answer the questions.
Students try to solve the same puzzle working in groups. Then students discuss questions about working individually versus working in groups.

> **Extension**
> Students research logic puzzles.
> - Ask students to work in groups researching copyright-free logic puzzles that they can copy, photocopy or download and print.
> - Invite students to compile their puzzles in an anthology and to share them with their classmates.

Wrap-up

Students role-play conversations about the Alma telescopes.
- Organize students into pairs and have them role-play a conversation about the Alma telescopes between a speaker from Group A and a speaker from Group B:
  » Group A: A news reporter, a high-school student interested in astronomy;
  » Group B: A Chilean astronomer, a foreign astronomer visiting the site.

➡ **(No homework today.)**

> **Teaching Tip**
> **Planning Activities**
> As a general rule, it is better to overplan a little for a lesson and to run out of time than to run short. It may be possible to recycle unused materials or activities in a subsequent lesson.

Project

Objective
Students will be able to prepare for a trip to Mars.

Lesson 9   Student's Book pp. 92 and 93

Warm-up
Students review their knowledge of the Solar System.
- In small groups, students brainstorm facts about the Solar System: the names of the planets, the order of the planets from the Sun, the relative sizes of the planets, etc.

1 Read the ad and complete the information.
Students read an ad for a trip to Mars and extract information from the reading to complete some notes.

Answers
top to bottom the Roman god of War, two, 24 hours and 37 minutes, 687 Earth days, 235 million kilometers, nine months

2 🎧²² Listen and label the objects on the next page.
Students listen and label a series of objects listed in the audio.

Audio Script
1. soccer ball
2. laptop
3. hamburgers
4. first aid kit
5. calendar
6. playing cards
7. handheld game
8. sewing kit
9. CDs
10. books
11. cans of soda
12. fruit
13. barbells
14. stationary bike

Wrap-up
Students write an ad for a trip to Earth.
- Have students reread the ad for the trip to Mars and review the pieces of information that it contains. Then ask students to imagine beings from some other planet reading an advertisement for a trip to Earth. Have them work in pairs to write an ad based on the ad for Mars, but about Earth.
- Invite students to share their ads with the rest of the class.

Lesson 10   Student's Book pp. 92 and 93

Warm-up
Students review the vocabulary items from the previous lesson in a game.
- Review the vocabulary from this page by playing Hangman.

3 **Work in groups. Follow the instructions.**
Students discuss items to take on a trip to Mars and prepare posters.
- Read aloud all the instructions. Then organize students into small groups and have them discuss the six most important items from the list on this page that they think they should take on a trip to Mars. For each item, have students think of an advantage and a disadvantage about taking that item to Mars.
- Have students prepare posters illustrating and explaining their six choices. Invite students to share their ideas with the rest of the class.

4 🎧²³ **Listen to an expert choose six items. Did you choose the same objects?**
Students listen to an expert's list and compare it with their own lists.

Audio Script
I'm Stacey and I'm an astronaut. Here are my suggestions for the trip to Mars.
Don't take the hamburgers. You need a freezer and you can't cook in space.
A soccer ball. That's fun, so yes. It's fun playing ball in zero gravity!
Soda cans. No. They explode in space and they can be dangerous.
First aid kit. Yes. That's useful in an emergency.
A handheld game is not a good idea. It needs lots of batteries.
Books. Yes, take them. You have lots of time to read in space!
A sewing kit. No. You use special clothes in space.
A laptop. No, because there is no Internet in space!
The exercise bike, yes! This is perfect for exercise on the spacecraft.
Music CDs. Yes, but choose music that everyone likes!
Fresh fruit and vegetables are only good for two or three days, so no.
A calendar. No. Why? The years are different on Mars.
Playing cards are a very good idea. There are hundreds of fun games to play.
Barbells. No. It looks like a good idea, but they weigh nothing in space!

The Digital Touch
To incorporate digital media in the project, suggest one or more of the following:
- Encourage students to use free downloadable poster-making programs for their posters.
- If possible, allow students to upload their work to the school's website.

Note that students should have the option to do a task on paper or digitally.

Wrap-up
Students compare posters and vote for their favorites.
- Invite students to vote for their favorite posters. There can be awards in various categories, e.g., best ideas and arguments, best layout and design, best use of technology, best overall poster, etc.

➡ **Workbook p. 148, Activity 1 (Review)**

Review

Objective
Students will be able to consolidate their understanding of the vocabulary and grammar learned in the unit.

Lesson 11   Student's Book p. 94

> ✔ **Homework Check!**
> Workbook p. 148, Activity 1 (Review)
> **Answers**
> 1 Answer the questions about a great vacation you had.
> Answers will vary.

Warm-up

Students review science projects from a previous lesson.
- With books closed, ask students to recall information about the two scientific projects covered on pages 84 and 85. Try to elicit some of the phrases used to describe the scientific method.

1 Complete the flowchart for the scientific method.
Students complete a flowchart summarizing the scientific method.

Answers
1. question, 2. research, 3. hypothesis, 4. experiment, 5. data, 6. conclusions

2 Choose the correct options to complete the sentences.
Students practice adjective–preposition combinations.

Answers
1. with, 2. about, 3. at, 4. in, 5. about, 6. about

3 Rewrite the sentences in the past simple.
Students practice the past simple in a rewriting exercise.

Answers
1. We cooked an omelet for lunch. 2. Did Fiona watch TV with you? 3. Adam didn't like the movie. 4. Denise and Joan didn't play volleyball. 5. Did you walk to school? 6. Chris looked tired.

> **Extension**
> Students create posters to illustrate the scientific method.
> - Organize students into small groups and have them design and create posters explaining the scientific method. They can use real-life projects or make up a their own examples to illustrate the method. Invite groups to share their finished work with the rest of the class.

Wrap-up

Students write affirmative, negative and interrogative sentences in the past simple.
- Have students work in threes. Students each write an affirmative sentence in the past simple on a sheet of paper. They pass their papers to the student on their left, who changes the sentence into the negative. Then students pass on their papers once more and change the sentence into a yes/no question.
- Ask groups of students to read aloud their sentences.

➡ **(No homework today.)**

> **Teaching Tip**
> **Personalizing Activities**
> Try as much as possible to make language activities more interesting and memorable by personalizing them. Refer to local people, places, events, traditions, etc. that students are familiar with and encourage students to use new language to express real ideas, opinions, information, etc. about their own lives.

Lesson 12   Student's Book p. 95

Warm-up

Students practice the past simple forms of irregular verbs.

- Conduct a quick-fire drill to practice past simple forms. Say a verb in its present base form and have students supply the past simple form. This can be conducted as a team game. Alternatively, do this as a dictation activity where you say a present verb and students have to write down the past simple form.

4 Complete the crossword with the past simple of these irregular verbs.

Students complete a crossword with the past simple forms of irregular verbs.

Answers

1. lost, 2. saw, 3. began, 4. wrote, 5. thought, 6. wore, 7. had, 8. drove, 9. made, 10. put, 11. did, 12. got, 13. chose, 14. spoke

5 Complete the interview with the correct forms of the verbs in parentheses.

Students read and complete an interview about the California Gold Rush with the past simple forms of the verbs provided.

Answers

1. was, 2. went, 3. did, begin, 4. discovered, 5. arrived, 6. wanted, 7. did, end, 8. ended, 9. did not / didn't find, 10. did not / didn't become, 11. lost, 12. got

6 Use the words below and add more to write sentences in the past that are true for you.

Students write true sentences in the past simple based on cues and personal information.

Answers

1. I met my best friend... , 2. I started school... , 3. This morning I ate ... for breakfast., 4. Yesterday I watched... on TV., 5. Last week I didn't... , 6. Last weekend I went...
Answers will vary.

Big Question

Students are given the opportunity to revisit the Big Question and reflect on it.

- Ask students to turn to the unit opener on page 83 and to look again at the image, which shows a light bulb and an explosion of bright colors.
- First, talk about the familiar image of the light bulb as a symbol for a new idea. Analyze the metaphorical association between a light bulb switching on and an idea suddenly "appearing" in a person's mind. Discuss the idea that a new idea illuminates what was previously in darkness, that is, ignorance or confusion.
- Ask students if they have experienced this type of "light bulb moment" and invite them to share details of the situation and how it felt when they "had" their bright idea or when the bright idea "came" to them.

Scorecard

Hand out (and/or project) a *Scorecard*. Have students fill in their *Scorecards* for this unit.

➤ Study for the unit test.

7 When is the right time?

Grammar

Future: will: It <u>will rain</u> tomorrow. It <u>will not be</u> cloudy today. <u>Will we have</u> snow this week?

Future: going to: <u>I'm going to go</u> the library. <u>They're not going to visit</u> their grandparents. <u>Are you going to buy</u> a new phone?

Short answers: Yes, it will.

Vocabulary

Weather: cloud, cloudy, fog, foggy, rain, rainy, snow, snowy, storm, stormy, sun, sunny, wind, windy

Reading

Previewing to predict content

Speaking

Storytelling

When is the right time?

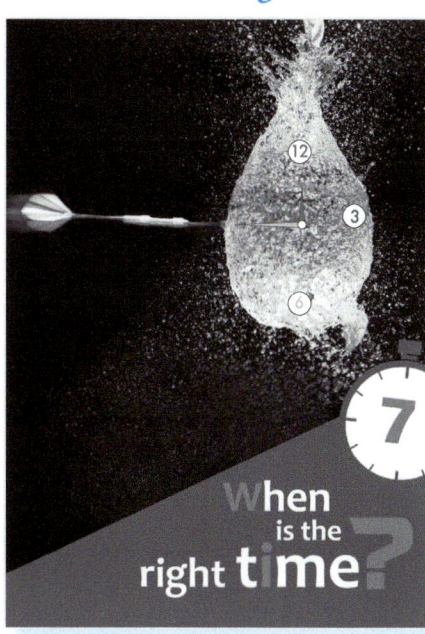

In the first lesson, read the unit title aloud and have students look carefully at the unit cover. Encourage them to think about the message in the picture. At the end of the unit, students will discuss the big question: *When is the right time?*

Teaching Tip

Promoting Feelings of Security

Offering challenges to learners is important, but challenges involve the risk of being wrong, and sometimes it is hard for learners to take this risk in public. Sometimes when students ask for reliable rules, this reflects their anxiety. Certain activities, for example, controlled practice, "rehearsals" in pairs or small groups, etc. can help learners feel safer. If you use interim rules, which evolve as learners' language develops, this can also be reassuring for learners.

Vocabulary

Objective
Students will be able to use **weather** vocabulary to talk about weather conditions and forecasts.

Lesson 1
Student's Book pp. 98 and 99

Warm-up

Students talk about and mime current and recent weather conditions.
- Say *Today is…* Then mime the weather, for example, *sunny* or *rainy*. Students may call out the words if they know them.
- Have students work in small groups. Tell them to act out the weather conditions for last week and for tomorrow.

1 Complete the chart using words in the weather forecast.
Students complete a noun–adjective chart with weather words.

Answers

1. snowy, 2. rainy, 3. fog, 4. cloudy, 5. sun, 6. windy, 7. storm

2 Complete the sentences using the adjectives in Activity 1.
Students complete sentences describing the situations in the pictures using weather adjectives.

Answers

1. foggy, 2. stormy, 3. snowy, 4. cloudy, 5. windy, 6. rainy, 7. sunny

> **Extension**
> Students create and present posters about the four seasons.
> - Organize students into groups and have them prepare illustrated posters about the four seasons.
> - Ask groups to present their posters by discussing the weather that is typical in each season.

Wrap-up

Students practice weather vocabulary in a miming game.
- Organize students into teams. A player from one team mimes an action to suggest a certain type of weather (for example, shivering with cold) and the members of the other team(s) have to guess the weather conditions.

➡ **Workbook p. 150, Activities 1 and 2**

> **Teaching Tip**
> **Preparing for Activities**
> Try to visualize the way a lesson or activity will go before you actually teach it. Consider how much time is required and what language students will need to successfully complete the activity. Imagine how it will come across from the students' point of view.

Lesson 2   Student's Book p. 99

> ✔ **Homework Check!**
> Workbook p. 150, Activities 1 and 2
> **Answers**
> **1 Find 6 weather words in the word snake.**
> snow, wind, rain, storm, fog, cloud
> **2 Write the missing letters to complete the weather words.**
> 1. wind, 2. fog, 3. rain, 4. sun, 5. clouds, 6. storm

Warm-up

Students talk about weather conditions that they like and dislike.

- As a small-group activity, invite students to share comments and opinions about the types of weather that they enjoy or don't enjoy, and why.

3 🎧²⁴ **Listen to the world weather forecast. Mark (✓) the weather you hear.**

Students listen to a weather forecast and identify types of weather.

Answers

Rome sunny, *Madrid* stormy, *London* foggy, *Berlin* cloudy, *Paris* cloudy, rainy, *Moscow* snowy

Audio Script

Now to weather around the world! It's spring in Europe and temperatures are very different across the continent. Starting in the South—it's very hot in Italy. It'll be 30 degrees Celsius and sunny all day in Rome. It will be a beautiful day! But not in Spain. It's stormy in most of Spain at the moment. But the storms will end in the early afternoon in Madrid. Moving north to England, it'll be a foggy, cold day in London. Let's look at Germany now. Berlin will be warm, 22 degrees but cloudy. It'll also be 22 degrees and cloudy in Paris, but it will rain later this afternoon. Finally, moving east to Russia, it's very cold there! It'll be about 1 degree below zero today and snowy. If you drive today, watch out for the snow in downtown Moscow! It's at least a meter deep! OK, that's all for now. Next weather update in an hour.

4 🎧²⁴ **Listen again and circle the mistake in each sentence. Rewrite the sentences.**

Students listen and then correct and rewrite sentences about the weather described in the forecast.

- Draw students' attention the *Guess What!* box. Read the information aloud and review the names of the four seasons. Elicit which months of the year each season corresponds to.

Answers

1. ~~Australia~~ It's spring in <u>Europe</u> and temperatures are very different across the continent. 2. ~~13~~ It'll be <u>30°</u> C and sunny all day in Rome. 3. ~~morning~~ The storms will end in the early <u>afternoon</u> in Madrid. 4. ~~warm~~ It's a foggy, <u>cold</u> day in London. 5. ~~rainy~~ Berlin will be warm, 22° C but <u>cloudy</u>. 6. ~~cloudy~~ It's <u>snowy</u> all over Moscow.

5 Think Fast! **What's the best time of year to visit your country?**

Students do a three-minute timed challenge: they discuss the most favorable climate conditions in their country.

- Organize students into groups and ask them to discuss the question. Then convene all the students in a whole-class discussion about the best time of year for tourists or other visitors to visit their country, in terms of the typical weather conditions.

Wrap-up

Students prepare their own weather forecasts.

- Organize students into pairs and invite them to prepare a weather forecast for a number of cities in their country for the next two or three days. If possible, provide students with relevant weather information for the last few days.

▶ **Workbook p. 150, Activity 3**

Grammar

Objectives
Students will be able use **future simple** with *will* for talking about predictions and *going to* for talking about plans in the future.

Lesson 3 Student's Book pp. 100 and 101

> ✔ **Homework Check!**
> Workbook p. 150, Activity 3
>
> **Answers**
> **3 Complete the messages with the words below.**
> 1. rainy, 2. cloudy, 3. foggy, 4. snowy, 5. sunny, 6. windy

Warm-up
Students recall the names of recent hurricanes.
- As a whole-class discussion, elicit the names of any recent hurricanes that students can remember. Invite them to share any information they have about recent hurricane events.

1 Read the forecast and trace the trajectory of the hurricane on the map.
Students read an account of a hurricane and trace its path on a map.
- Draw students' attention to the *Guess What!* box. Read the information aloud and elicit or provide the names of some notable recent hurricanes or storms in your region of the world.

2 Complete the sentences using *will* or *won't*.
Students complete sentences in future simple with the correct verb form.

Answers
1. will, 2. won't, 3. will, 4. will, 5. will, 6. won't

3 Read and complete the sentences with the future simple.
Students complete sentences with the correct future verb form.

Answers
1. will get, 2. Will, be, 3. Will, win, 4. will be, 5. won't go, 6. will have

> **Extension**
> - Organize students into groups and invite them to find out about a notable hurricane or storm. Tell them to produce a map showing the trajectory of the hurricane and to write a newspaper article about the effects of the storm on towns and cities in the area.

Wrap-up
Students interview each other using future simple.
- Students form pairs. Student A will be the interviewer, and Student B will be a hurricane expert.
- Tell students that Hurricane Bob is approaching the Gulf of Mexico, moving between Cuba and Florida.
- Using the map on page 100 and the interview in Activity 1 as a model, tell students to interview each other about the effects of Hurricane Bob.
- If time permits, have students switch roles and interview each other again.

➡ **Workbook p. 151, Activities 1 and 2**

🐝 Teaching Tip
Using Student Knowledge
When a student asks the meaning of a word, don't automatically reply. First, ask the class if anyone can explain it.

Lesson 4   Student's Book p. 101

> ✔ **Homework Check!**
> Workbook p. 151, Activities 1 and 2
> **Answers**
> **1 Complete the conversation using future with *will*.**
> 1. will not / won't know, 2. will meet, 3. will make, 4. will not / won't like, 5. will not / won't be, 6. will start, 7. will help
> **2 Use the words to make predictions.**
> 1. She will not / won't tell anyone. 2. The vet will know what's wrong. 3. You will not / won't find any pictures of me. 4. Everyone will love it. 5. We will win a lot of money in the future.

Warm-up
Students make predictions using *will* and *won't*.
- Set a time limit of, say, three minutes and tell students to write six predictions, three using *will* and three with *won't*, about current events (politics, sports, entertainment, etc.) in their country. Invite students to share their predictions.

4 Read the post and complete the mind map.
Students read about people's plans and use the information to complete a mind map.

Answers
PJ stay, board up windows, *me* Answers will vary.
Silvia go to sister's house

5 Read the notes and write plans using *going to*.
Students write full sentences using *going to* to express plans indicated in notes.

Answers
1. Simone is going to call her grandma on Friday. 2. Donnie and I are going to have a music lesson after school. 3. Dad is going to fly from New York to Chicago on Saturday. 4. Bobby and Helen are going to watch American Idol tonight.

6 Write the sentences in Activity 5 in negative and interrogative forms in your notebook.
Students convert affirmative sentences into negative and interrogative forms.

Answers
1. Simone is not going to call her grandma on Friday. Is Simone going to call her grandma on Friday? 2. Donnie and I are not going to have a music lesson after school. Are Donnie and I going to have a music lesson after school? 3. Dad is not going to fly from New York to Chicago on Saturday. Is Dad going to fly from New York to Chicago on Saturday? 4. Bobby and Helen are not going to watch American Idol tonight. Are Bobby and Helen going to watch American Idol tonight?

Wrap-up
Students exchange information about their plans.
- Organize students into pairs or threes and have them exchange information about their plans using *going to*. Invite students to share their findings with the rest of the class.

▶ **Workbook pp. 151 and 152, Activities 3–5**

Reading & Speaking

Objectives
Students will be able to preview a text to predict the content. They will also be able to tell stories.

Lesson 5 Student's Book pp. 102 and 103

✔ **Homework Check!**
Workbook pp. 151 and 152, Activities 3–5
Answers
3 Complete the future plans using *going to*. There's an extra verb you don't need.
1. is going to sing, 2. is going to dance, 3. am not / 'm not going to be, 4. are not / aren't going to speak, 5. are going to play
4 Look at the form and answer the questions in your notebook.
1. She's going to learn Chinese. 2. She's going to play baseball. 3. Yes, she is. 4. She is going to go horse riding. 5. No, she isn't.
5 Cross out one extra word in each dialogue.
1. to, 2. don't, 3. be, 4. no, 5. 's

Warm-up
Students talk about strange weather stories and weather expressions.
- Ask *Do you know the expression "It's raining cats and dogs"? What do you think it means?* Elicit ideas.

1 Look at the title and the pictures. Answer the questions.
Students look just at certain items of a text and make predictions about its content.
- Draw students' attention to the **Be Strategic!** box. Read the information aloud and encourage students to look carefully at the title, layout, pictures, graphics, etc. of a text before reading it.

Answers
1. a newspaper article, 2. spiders, 3. rain, wind, snow

2 Read the article and underline evidence to prove these facts.
Students scan a text to look for specific information.
Answers
1. a strange feeling in his ear, 2. is an arachnophobe, 3. the next morning, the whole town was white, 4. use these parachutes to travel in the wind, 5. a very rare event

Wrap-up
Students share their reactions to the news article.
- As a whole-class activity, recap the article and elicit reactions, observations and comments.

➡ **Workbook p. 153, Activity 1**

Lesson 6 — Student's Book pp. 102 and 103

> ✔ **Homework Check!**
> Workbook p. 153, Activity 1
> **Answers**
> **1 Look at the pictures and the titles. Mark (✓) a–d if you think the article will mention them. Then read and check.**
> a, c, d

Warm-up

Students listen and check factual information from the newspaper article.

- Read aloud a series of sentences about the newspaper article on the previous page, some true and some false. Have students listen and call out when they hear a false statement. Ask them to correct the false information.

3 Read the article again quickly and write down eight key words. Retell the story using your key words.

Students summarize and retell the story in the article using key words.

Answers
Answers will vary.

4 Talk about an unusual day. Follow these guidelines.

Students talk about unusual days that they have experienced in the context of extreme or unusual weather.

Stop and Think! Critical Thinking

How does different weather affect your behavior or your feelings?

- Organize students into small groups and have them discuss the question. (If necessary, write some ideas on the board to get them started.)
- Invite groups to share their ideas with the rest of the class.

Wrap-up

Students write a personal account of an experience of extreme or unusual weather.

- Invite students to use their oral presentations from Activity 4 as the basis for a written account of their experience of extreme or unusual weather.

▶ **Workbook p. 153, Activity 2**

Preparing for the Next Lesson
Ask students to watch a video about visiting Switzerland: goo.gl/AG2yot.

Culture

Objectives
Students will be able to talk about Switzerland. They will also be able to discuss the importance of punctuality in different cultures.

Lesson 7 Student's Book pp. 104 and 105

> ✔ **Homework Check!**
> Workbook p. 153, Activity 2
> **Answers**
> **2 Match the information with the paragraph in the article. There is an extra option.**
> *top to bottom* 3, 4, [none], 1, 5, 2

Warm-up
Students share basic geographical knowledge about Switzerland.
- As a whole-class activity, elicit some basic facts about Switzerland (its location, its approximate area and population in relation to the students' own country, its landscape, etc.).

1 🎧²⁵ **Read and guess which two facts are false. Then listen and check.**
Students read facts about Switzerland and guess which two statements are false.

Answers
1 and 4

Audio Script
Two facts are false.
Number 1 is false. The capital city of Switzerland is Bern. Number 4 is false. Several European countries don't use the euro, including Switzerland. Switzerland's currency is the Swiss Franc.

2 Read the blog introduction quickly and complete the sentences. Then answer the question.
Students read a text and obtain some general information. They use the information from the reading to complete the sentences and answer the question.

Answers
1. Switzerland, Swiss, 2. lived, 3. St. Gallen, Switzerland, 4. She has gotten used to life in the United States.

3 Underline three examples of Swiss punctuality in the blog. Explain why Nicole is not happy about them.
Students scan a text for specific information.

Answers

1. If you have a party at 8:00 p.m., everyone arrives on time. Her family is not ready for the guests to arrive on time. 2. If the timetable says the bus leaves at 13:43, it leaves at exactly 13:43. She misses her train when she arrives at the station a minute or two late. 3. Everyone has their coffee break and lunch at exactly the same time. There are always big lines at coffee shops when everyone has their break.

Extension
Students discuss reverse culture shock.
- Organize students into small groups. Tell them to imagine that they have just returned to their own country after living away for five years. Have them describe the things that they would find most difficult to readjust to.

Wrap-up
Students role-play a conversation.
- Organize students into pairs and have them role-play a conversation in which Nicole explains to a Swiss friend the things that she is having to learn all over again after her return to Switzerland.

⏩ **(No homework today.)**

Lesson 8   Student's Book pp. 104 and 105

Warm-up
Students recap information about Switzerland.
- With books closed, carry out a quick-fire quiz to review basic facts about Switzerland from page 104.

4 Complete the definitions using the highlighted words in the blog.
Students complete definitions of key vocabulary items from the text.

Answers

1. timetable, 2. break, 3. punctual, 4. knock,
5. tweak

5 Mark (✓) the sentences that are true for you. Are you like people in Switzerland?
Students compare and contrast cultures.

Answers

Answers will vary.

6 Write a comment to Nicole's blog about punctuality where you live. Choose one of these situations.
Students write a comment to post to Nicole's blog about punctuality in their own country in a specific situation.

Answers

Answers will vary.

Stop and Think! Value
Is punctuality important in your culture? When is it most important to be on time?
- Organize students into small groups and have them discuss the question. (If necessary, write some ideas on the board to get them started.)
- Invite groups to share their ideas with the rest of the class.

Wrap-up
Students come up with sentences using key vocabulary items.
- Students form pairs. Student A chooses a word from the highlighted words in the blog on page 104 or the glossary words on page 105. As quickly as possible, Student B uses the word in a sentence. Then Student B picks a word for Student A to use in a sentence.

➡ **(No homework today.)**

Project

Objective
Students will be able to create a motivational poster giving suggestions or advice.

Lesson 9   Student's Book pp. 106 and 107

Warm-up
Students talk about what makes them feel calm.
- As a whole-class activity, invite students to discuss the sorts of things that can make them feel stressed and the things that help them to feel calm.

1 Look at the poster. Answer the questions.
Students look at a poster and discuss questions about it.

Answers

Answers will vary.

2 Match the problems with the suggestions. Which one is the most useful for you?
Students discuss time management problems and possible solutions.
- Tell students to look at the activity. Elicit that all of the problems are related to time management. Have students work in pairs, first matching each problem with a solution and then discussing which suggestions are most useful for them. Check answers and discuss as a whole class.

Answers

1. b, 2. c, 3. d, 4. e, 5. a

3 Summarize the suggestions in Activity 2 and place them in the corresponding posters on page 107. Use three words maximum.
Students summarize ideas in short phrases and match them to poster designs.

Answers

Answers will vary.
Suggestion a. *Poster* 5, b. 1, c. 2, d. 3, e. 4

Wrap-up
Students choose their favorites from the posters on page 107.
- Conduct a quick show-of-hands vote to determine which of the posters on page 107 is the students' favorite. Encourage them to say why they like a certain poster more than another.

Lesson 10   Student's Book pp. 106 and 107

Warm-up
Students discuss the popularity and usefulness of motivational posters.
- Write the following questions on the board: *Where are motivational posters often displayed? Why do you think they are so popular nowadays? What effects are they intended to have? How much effect do motivational posters have on you?*
- Organize students into small groups and ask students to discuss the questions.

4 Read and make suggestions using *should*.
Students consider questions about school habits and lifestyle and make suggestions using *should*.

Answers

Answers will vary.

5 Make a poster. Follow these guidelines.
Students make motivational posters.

Extension
Students prepare a presentation about motivational posters.
- Organize students into small groups and invite them to research and prepare an oral presentation about motivational posters that are freely accessible online. Suggest to students that they choose a particular quality or virtue, for example, Determination, Teamwork, Focus, etc. and find posters that illustrate that idea.

The Digital Touch
To incorporate digital media in the project, suggest one or more of the following:
- Encourage students to use free downloadable poster-making programs for their posters.
- If possible, allow students to upload their work to the school's website.

Note that students should have the option to do a task on paper or digitally.

Wrap-up
Students compare posters and vote for their favorites.
- Invite students to vote for their favorite motivational posters. There can be awards in various categories, e.g., best ideas and phrase, best layout and design, best use of technology, best overall poster, etc.

➡ **Workbook p. 152, Activity 1 (Review)**

Teaching Tip
Making Mistakes
Don't get upset if once in a while you cannot answer a difficult grammar question or if you make the occasional spelling mistake. This happens to nearly all teachers. It is perfectly fine to say to students, *Let me think about that. I'll make a note and get back to you tomorrow.* It is better to take a careful look at the topic and prepare a clear explanation than to get flustered and give an incorrect answer.

Review

Objective
Students will be able to consolidate their understanding of the vocabulary and grammar learned in the unit.

Lesson 11 Student's Book p. 108

> ✔ **Homework Check!**
> Workbook p. 152, Activity 1 (Review)
>
> **Answers**
> **1 Look at this weekly planner. Write sentences in your notebook.**
> 1. I'm going to take my dog to the vet on Tuesday.
> 2. I'm going to go to the library on Wednesday.
> 3. I'm going to take an English test on Thursday.
> 4. I'm going to go rollerblading with friends on Friday. 5. I'm going to go swimming with friends on Saturday. 6. I'm going to visit my grandparents on Sunday.

Warm-up
Students review weather vocabulary playing a game.
• Review weather vocabulary from page 98 (snow, cloudy, fog, sunny, etc.) by playing Hangman.

1 Match the sentence parts.
Students practice weather vocabulary by matching sentence halves.

Answers
1. c, 2. g, 3. e, 4. a, 5. f, 6. d, 7. b

2 Look at the icons and complete using adjectives.
Students complete sentences with the correct weather adjectives using weather icons as cues.

Answers
1. stormy, 2. foggy, 3. cloudy, 4. sunny, 5. rainy, 6. windy, 7. snowy

3 Circle the correct options to complete the conversation.
Students read and complete a conversation in future simple with the correct verb forms.

Answers
1. Will, 2. won't, 3. will be, 4. won't, 5. give, 6. won't

Wrap-up
Students make predictions about events in the school calendar.
• Organize students into pairs and have them come up with a series of predictions for events in the school calendar. They can include, for example, the results of exams, the outcome of school sports tournaments, school festivals and celebrations, etc.
• Invite students to share their ideas with the rest of the class.

➡ **(No homework today.)**

Lesson 12   Student's Book p. 109

Warm-up

Students review the form of *going to*.
- Write on the board a series of sentence prompts such as the following: my mom / look for a new job, my friends / go to the movies, etc. Have students construct a complete sentence from each prompt, using the correct form of *going to*.

4 Complete the conversation using future with *going to*.

Students read and complete a conversation with the correct forms of *going to*.

Answers

1. are, going to do, 2. are going to drive, 3. are, going to travel, 4. am going to show, 5. are going to start, 6. are not going to visit, 7. Am, going to see, 8. are going to spend, 9. is going to drive, 10. are, going to sleep

5 Circle one mistake in each sentence. Then rewrite the sentences.

Students correct sentences with mistakes in the future simple or future with *going to*.

Answers

1. ~~coming~~ How many people will <u>come</u> to the party? 2. ~~doesn't~~ It <u>won't</u> snow tomorrow. 3. ~~go~~ My brother is <u>going</u> to learn to drive next week. 4. ~~Are~~ <u>Am</u> I going to be in your class next year? 5. ~~don't~~ Sally <u>isn't</u> going to go on the school trip tomorrow. 6. ~~Do we will~~ <u>Will we</u> have any exams next year?

6 Complete the agenda, using your own information.

In a personalization activity, students complete an agenda with weather predictions and plans.

Answers

Answers will vary.

❓ Big Question

Students are given the opportunity to revisit the Big Question and reflect on it.
- Ask students to turn to the unit opener on page 97 and to look again at the image. Discuss how this remarkable photo was taken at exactly the right time—precise to within a fraction of a second—to capture the instant in which the dart punctured the water-filled balloon.
- Talk about how certain human activities depend on people, machines, systems, etc. all operating efficiently and punctually. Elicit examples of activities where punctuality and timing are paramount, for example, air travel, a military operation, etc.

⭐ Scorecard

Hand out (and/or project) a *Scorecard*. Have students fill in their *Scorecards* for this unit.

➡ **Study for the unit test.**

8 How do you feel?

Grammar

Questions: <u>Where</u> do you live? <u>How much</u> is it? <u>What</u> is his name?

What and Which: <u>What</u> would you like to eat? <u>Which</u> flight is ours?

Vocabulary

Feelings: anger, angry, embarrassment, embarrassed, excitement, excited, fear, frightened, happiness, happy, jealousy, jealous, sadness, sad, worry, worried

Writing

Expressing opinions in a review essay

Speaking

Discussing movie reviews

How do you feel?

In the first lesson, read the unit title aloud and have students look carefully at the unit cover. Encourage them to think about the message in the picture. At the end of the unit, students will discuss the big question: *How do you feel?*

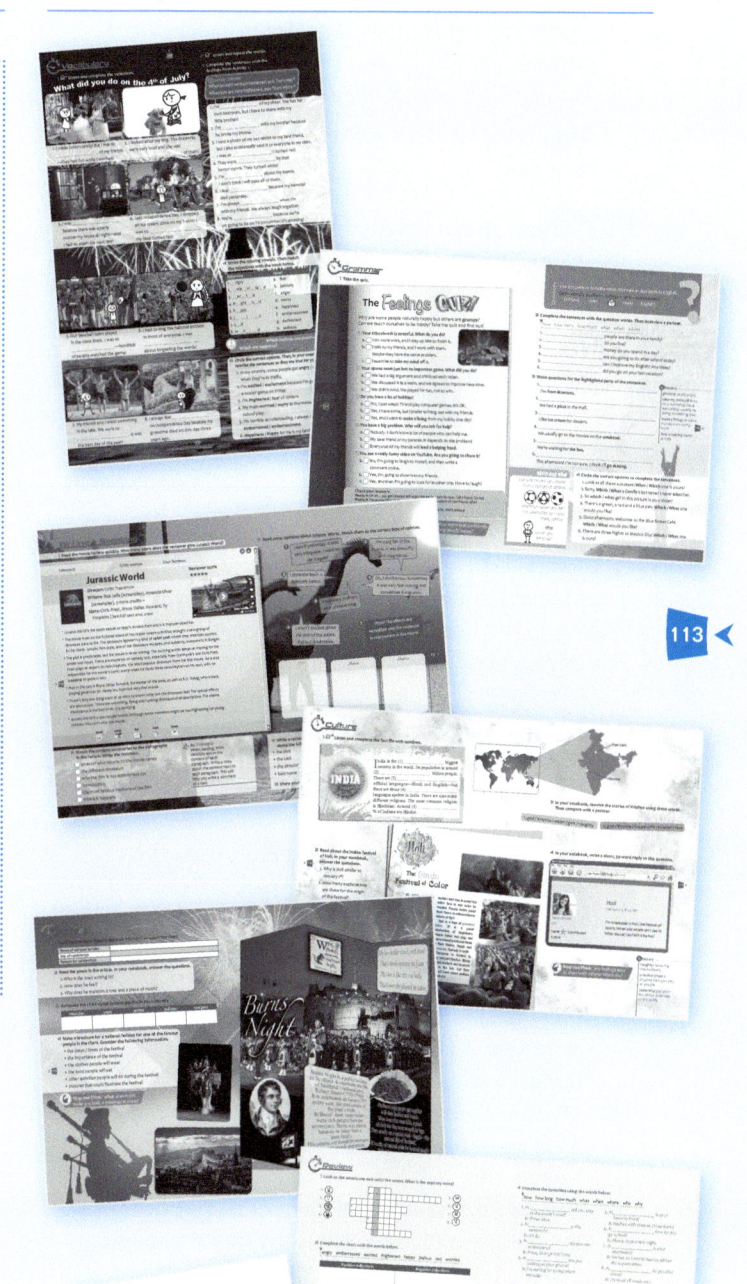

Teaching Tip

Getting Feedback from Students

Getting feedback from students about your classes can give you valuable insight into not only your teaching, but also your students. One way is to conduct a multiple-choice survey, asking them what they enjoy doing, what helps them learn, what they're excited about after class, etc. After reviewing students' answers, integrate their ideas into your lessons or even guide a brainstorming session on how these ideas could be used in class.

Vocabulary

Objective
Students will be able to use **feelings** vocabulary to talk about their emotions.

Lesson 1
Student's Book pp. 112 and 113

Warm-up
Students discuss the theme of feelings and where they come from.
- As a small-group activity, students talk about where we feel feelings. Ask *Are feelings more like thoughts or physical sensations? In which parts of the body do we experience emotions?*
- Groups report their answers to the questions to the class.

1 🎧²⁶ **Listen and complete the sentences.**
Students practice feelings vocabulary in a listening activity.

Answers
1. jealous, 2. frightened, 3. angry, 4. embarrassed, 5. excited, 6. worried, 7. happy, 8. sad

Audio Script
1. I made cotton candy! But I was so jealous of my friends—they had fun while I worked! Jealous. J-E-A-L-O-U-S
2. I looked after my dog. The fireworks were very loud and she was frightened of them! Frightened. F-R-I-G-H-T-E-N-E-D
3. I was angry because there was a party outside my house all night—and I had an exam the next day! Angry. A-N-G-R-Y
4. Last Independence Day, I dropped an ice cream cone on my T-shirt! I was so embarrassed my face turned red! Embarrassed. E-M-B-A-R-R-A-S-S-E-D
5. Our baseball team played in the state finals. I was so excited—hundreds of people watched the game! Excited. E-X-C-I-T-E-D
6. I had to sing the national anthem in front of everyone. I was worried about forgetting the words! Worried. W-O-R-R-I-E-D
7. My friends and I went swimming in the lake. We were so happy. It was the best day of the year! Happy. H-A-P-P-Y
8. I always feel sad on Independence Day because my grandma died on this day three years ago. Sad. S-A-D

2 🎧²⁷ **Listen and repeat the words.**
Students listen and repeat vocabulary items.

Audio Script
1. jealous
2. angry
3. embarrassed
4. frightened
5. worried
6. sad
7. happy
8. excited

3 **Complete the sentences with the feelings from Activity 1.**
Students use the correct feelings vocabulary to complete sentences.
- Draw students' attention to the **Guess What!** box. Read the information aloud and explain these expressions. Ask students if they have similar expressions in their own language.

Answers
1. jealous, 2. angry, 3. embarrassed, 4. frightened, 5. worried, 6. sad, 7. happy, 8. excited

Wrap-up
Students form pairs to share their own sentences about feelings. Write on the board *I feel frightened when… I feel happy when…* Set a stopwatch for two minutes. Have pairs race to think of as many ways to complete the sentences as possible. Then have pairs share their sentences with the class.

➡ **Workbook p. 154, Activities 1 and 2**

Lesson 2 Student's Book p. 113

✔ **Homework Check!**

Workbook p. 154, Activities 1 and 2

Answers

1 Write the missing letters to complete the words.
1. frightened, 2. happy, 3. sad, 4. angry, 5. jealous, 6. worried, 7. embarrassed

2 Cross out the word that doesn't belong.
1. excited, 2. sad, 3. excited, 4. angry, 5. happy

Warm-up

Students review feelings vocabulary by playing Charades.

- Organize students into teams. Have pairs of teams play together. Tell each team to make a set of eight cards, with one feelings adjective on each card: *angry, embarrassed, excited, frightened, happy, jealous, sad, worried*.

- Teams take turns. One student from each team draws a card and acts out the feelings word. His or her team tries to guess which word it is. The team of each pair of teams with the most correct guesses wins.

4 Write the missing vowels. Then match the adjectives with the noun forms.

Students complete adjectives with missing vowels and then match adjectives with related nouns.

Answers

1. angry, c, 2. embarrassed, f, 3. excited, g, 4. frightened, a, 5. happy, e, 6. jealous, b, 7. sad, h, 8. worried, d

5 Think Fast! Which feelings are positive? Which are negative?

Students do a three-minute timed challenge: they determine which feelings are positive and which are negative.

Answers

positive happiness, excitement
negative fear, jealousy, anger, worry, embarrassment, sadness

6 Circle the correct options. Then, in your notebook, rewrite the sentences so they are true for you.

Students select adjectives or nouns to complete sentences. They then personalize the sentences.

Answers

1. angry, 2. excited, 3. frightened, 4. worry, 5. embarrassed, 6. Happiness, Answers will vary.

Extension

Students design and create feelings posters.

- Organize students into groups and invite them to design and create illustrated posters showing feelings adjectives (sad, worried, etc.) and their corresponding abstract nouns (sadness, worry, etc.)

- Display students' posters around the classroom.

Wrap-up

Students use feelings adjectives and nouns in sentences.

- Students form pairs. Student A says a feelings adjective or noun. Student B uses the corresponding adjective or noun in a sentence.

- Give students an example: A: *frightened*. B: *My cat has a terrible fear of dogs*.

- Then students switch roles and continue until they have made sentences with all of the vocabulary words.

▶ **Workbook p. 154, Activity 3**

> **Teaching Tip**
>
> **Giving Students Time to Think**
> During class, remember to give students enough time to listen, think and process their thoughts so that they can then ask something or speak. While giving them time to think, resist the temptation to talk!

Grammar

Objectives
Students will be able to use **Wh- words** to ask **information questions**. They will also be able to use *what* and *which* to ask questions about options.

Lesson 3   Student's Book pp. 114 and 115

✔ **Homework Check!**
Workbook p. 154, Activity 3

Answers
3 Complete the sentences with the noun forms of the words in parentheses.
1. excitement, 2. jealousy, 3. sadness, 4. anger, 5. embarrassment, 6. happiness

Warm-up
Students review yes/no questions.
- Write on the board scrambled versions of yes/no questions from the quiz on this page, for example, *you / Do / a / of / have / hobbies? / lot* and have students unscramble them.

1 Take the quiz.
Students answer a quiz about feelings.

Answers
Answers will vary.

Stop and Think! Critical Thinking
> 116

How important are friends and family in keeping people happy?
- Organize students into small groups and have them discuss the question. Tell students to start by completing the sentence *I feel happy when...* with ideas about friends and family.
- Have students summarize the ideas about how family and friends contribute to their happiness they brainstormed through the sentence completion activity.
- Invite groups to share their ideas with the rest of the class.

2 Complete the sentences with the question words. Then interview a partner.
Students complete questions with the correct question words and then ask each other the questions.
- Tell students to look at the box at the top of the page. Talk through the structure. If necessary, write a couple of sentences on the board and highlight the key parts of the structure.

Answers
1. How many, 2. Where, 3. How much, 4. What, 5. How, 6. Where

Wrap-up
Students write additional questions from Activity 2.
- Have students write a supplementary question for each item in Activity 1. For example, after question 3, *How much money do you spend in a day?*, a student could ask *What do you spend it on?*
- Students ask their partners their follow-up questions.

➡ **Workbook p. 155, Activities 1 and 2**

Lesson 4 Student's Book pp. 114 and 115

> ✔ **Homework Check!**
> Workbook p. 155, Activities 1 and 2
> **Answers**
> **1 Complete the interview using the questions.**
> 1. What is it about? 2. When did it start? 3. Who are the actors in it? 4. Why do you like it? 5. How long is the show?
> **2 Write yes/no questions.**
> 1. Is Hank going to visit us tomorrow? 2. Does Tom usually do judo after school? 3. Did your mom drive you to school yesterday? 4. Is the baby sleeping at the moment? 5. Is there any milk in the fridge?

Warm-up
Students distinguish between yes/no questions and *Wh-* questions.
- Write on the board a selection of questions and ask students to say which ones are yes/no questions and which ones are *Wh-* questions.

3 Write questions for the highlighted parts of the sentences.
Students use the prompts in sentences to write questions that correspond to the answer given.

Answers
1. Where are you from? 2. What did you have to eat? / What did you eat? 3. What do you like to eat for dessert? / What do you like for dessert? 4. When do you usually go to the movies? 5. What are you waiting for? 6. What are you going to do this afternoon?

4 Circle the correct options to complete the sentences.
Students select the correct question word to complete each sentence.
- Draw students' attention to the **Which** *and* **What** box. Read the information aloud. Elicit a few examples.

Answers
1. Which, 2. What, 3. which, 4. Which, 5. What, 6. Which

Wrap-up
Students improvise conversations from the questions in Activity 4.
- Read aloud the correct version of item 1 in Activity 4 (Which one is yours?). First elicit where a person might be asking this question (at an airport, in a hotel, etc.) and then elicit a series of possible answers to the question. Have students work in pairs improvising short exchanges based on the questions in the activity.

⏵ **Workbook p. 156, Activity 3**

> 💭 **Teaching Tip**
> **Modeling Improvised Conversations**
> Improvised conversations, dialogues and role-plays are great ways to gain more fluency in recently-learned language by using it in relatable contexts. However, students may be hesitant to start. It's a good idea to model a sample conversation so students have a concrete example of what's expected of them.

Writing & Speaking

Objectives
Students will be able to express opinions in a movie review. They will also be able to discuss movie reviews.

Lesson 5   Student's Book p. 116

> ✔ Homework Check!
> Workbook p. 156, Activity 3
>
> **Answers**
> **3 Circle the correct options to complete the conversation.**
> 1. Which, 2. Which, 3. What, 4. What, 5. Which, 6. Which, 7. What

Warm-up

Students discuss movies that they have seen recently.
- As a small-group activity, have students discuss movies that they have seen recently. Encourage them to comment on movies that they enjoyed and also on movies that they found disappointing.

1 Read the movie review quickly. How many stars does the reviewer give *Jurassic World*?

Students skim through a movie review and identify how many stars the movie got.

Answer

▶ 118   Five stars

2 Match the content summaries to the paragraphs in the review. Write the numbers.

Students match sentences with the paragraphs in the review they summarize.
- Draw students' attention to the **Be Strategic!** box. Read the information aloud and encourage students to develop the technique of writing a brief content note next to each paragraph, which will help them write summaries of texts.

Answers

top to bottom paragraph 4, paragraph 5, paragraph 6, paragraph 1, paragraph 3, paragraph 2

Wrap-up

Students share opinions about *Jurassic World* or other, similar movies.
- Organize students into small groups and invite them to exchange opinions about either this movie or other, similar movies that all the members of the group have seen. Encourage groups to organize their opinions in topic areas like the summary sentences in Activity 2. Have groups share their views with the class.

➡ **Workbook p. 157, Activities 1 and 2**

Lesson 6   Student's Book p. 117

> ✔ **Homework Check!**
> Workbook p. 157, Activities 1 and 2
>
> **Answers**
> **1 Read the book review. How many stars does the review give the book?**
> Three and a half stars
> **Mark (✓) the correct options.**
> 1. a, 2. b, 3. a, 4. c

Warm-up
Students brainstorm adjectives to use in a movie review.
- With books closed, ask students to write a list of adjectives in small groups that they could use to describe an action movie. Prompt them to think of ways of describing the plot of the film, a particular scene, the way an actor acts, a special effect, etc.

3 Read some opinions about Jurassic World. Match them to the correct type of opinion.
Students sort opinions into categories (positive, neutral, negative).

Answers
Positive 1, 2, 7 *Negative* 3, 5 *Neutral* 4, 6

4 Write a review about a movie you know.
Students write movie reviews.

Answers
Answers will vary.

5 Share your reviews in small groups. Decide what movie to see.
Students share their reviews and vote for the movies they would like to see most.

> ### Extension
> Students create scripts for movie trailers.
> - Organize students into small groups and have them write scripts and storyboards for trailers for a movie that they know and like or even for a made-up movie of their own invention.
> - Invite groups to share their work with the rest of the class.

Wrap-up
Students play a guessing game about famous movies.
- Organize students into teams. A player from one team describes a famous movie (without mentioning the title), referring to elements of the plot, the main characters or the actors who play them, a memorable scene, etc. for the other team(s) to guess.

➡ **Workbook p. 157, Activity 3**

Preparing for the Next Lesson
Ask students to watch an introductory video about the Holi festival in India: goo.gl/qLbbw0.

Culture

> **Objectives**
> Students will be able to talk about the Holi festival in India. They will also be able to discuss the diversity of religious and social festivals around the world.

Lesson 7 — Student's Book pp. 118 and 119

> ✔ **Homework Check!**
> Workbook p. 157, Activity 3
> Answers
> **3 Write a review of a comic book, graphic novel or book.**
> Answers will vary.

Warm-up

Students brainstorm the names of religious festivals.
- As a whole-group activity, ask students to brainstorm the names of festivals and celebrations from a variety of religions, for example, Ramadan, Hanukkah, Easter, Diwali, etc. Write suggestions on the board.

1 🎧²⁸ **Listen and complete the fact file with numbers.**
Students listen and complete a fact file with numbers from the audio.

Answers

1. second, 2. 1.2, 3. two, 4. 780, 5. 80

Audio Script

India is the second biggest country in the world. Its population is around 1.2 billion people. There are two official languages—Hindi and English—but there are about 780 languages spoken in India. There are also many different religions. The most common religion is Hinduism. Around 80% of Indians are Hindus.

2 Read about the Indian festival of Holi. In your notebook, answer the questions.
Students read a text and find specific information in it to answer questions.

Answers

1. It is the start of the Hindu new year. 2. Two, 3. Happiness, 4. The article says that people dance and sing. 5. No, everyone is invited to play. 6. People are covered with colored paint.

Wrap-up

Students share their impressions of the Holi festival.
- As a whole-class activity, invite students to share their impressions of the Holi festival. Ask them if they think that they would enjoy taking part in the festival and why, or why not.

➡ **(No homework today.)**

Lesson 8   Student's Book pp. 118 and 119

Warm-up
Students recap information about the Holi festival.
- Students form pairs and take turns asking each other questions about Holi.

3 In your notebook, rewrite the stories of Krishna using these words. Then compare with a partner.
Students rewrite two key stories from the article about Holi using cues.

Answers

Answers will vary.

4 In your notebook, write a short, 50-word reply to this question.
Students write a short reply to a question about Holi.

Answers

Answers will vary.

> ### Extension
> Students create posters about religious festivals and celebrations.
> - Organize students into small groups and invite them to design and create an information poster about a religious festival or celebration from another country.
> - Have students display their work around the classroom.

Stop and Think! Value
Are feelings easy to share with others? Which are?
- Organize students into small groups and have them discuss the question. Tell students to remember which feelings they classified as negative and which as positive.
- Invite groups to share their ideas with the rest of the class.

Wrap-up
Students role-play conversations about a festival in their own country.
- Organize students into pairs and have them role-play conversations in which a visitor from another country asks a resident about a local or national festival.
- Invite pairs of students to share their role plays with the rest of the class.

➡ **(No homework today.)**

Project

Objective
Students will be able to create a brochure.

Lesson 9   Student's Book pp. 120 and 121

Warm-up
Students talk about their favorite festivals and celebrations.
- As a whole-class activity, invite students to talk about their favorite festivals and celebrations in their own country.
- Note the celebrations students mention on the board and hold a class vote for students' favorite celebration or festival.

1 Read the brochure about a national holiday. Complete the chart.

Students read a brochure and complete a chart with information from the text.

Answers
top to bottom Burns Night, January 25th, To celebrate the life of Scotland's national poet, Robert Burns

2 Read the poem in the article. In your notebook, answer the questions.

Students read part of a poem and answer questions about it.
- Tell students to read the four lines of the poem (the first verse of a four-verse poem by Burns called *A Red, Red Rose*).

Answers
Answers will vary.

Wrap-up
Students discuss their impressions of Burns Night.
- As a whole class, invite students to share their impressions of Burns Night. Referring to details and photos in the brochure (the music, the food, etc.), ask students whether they think they would enjoy participating in a Burns Night celebration and why, or why not.

Lesson 10   Student's Book pp. 120 and 121

Warm-up
Students recap information about Burns Night.
- With books closed, recap the key points of the brochure about Burns Night. Either ask straightforward questions such as *Who was Robert Burns?* or make true/false statements and have students identify and correct the false statements.

3 Complete the chart about famous people in your country.
Students complete a chart about notable artists, writers, etc. from their country.

Answers
Answers will vary.

4 Make a brochure for a national holiday for one of the famous people in the chart. Consider the following information.
Students create a brochure for a national celebration in honor of a famous artist, musician, poet, etc.

Stop and Think! Critical Thinking
What does music make you feel? A painting? A poem?
- Organize students into small groups and have them discuss the question. Encourage students to talk about a favorite song, painting or poem. (If necessary, write some ideas on the board to get them started.)
- Invite groups to share their ideas with the rest of the class.

The Digital Touch
To incorporate digital media in the project, suggest one or more of the following:
- Encourage students to use free downloadable brochure-design programs for their brochures.
- If possible, allow students to upload their work to the school's website.

Note that students should have the option to do a task on paper or digitally.

Wrap-up
Students compare brochures and vote for their favorites.
- Invite students to vote for their favorite brochures. There can be awards in various categories, e.g., most original ideas, best layout and design, best use of technology, best overall brochure, etc.

▶ **Workbook p. 156, Activity 1 (Review)**

> **Teaching Tip**
> **Helping Students Personalize Lessons**
> Try to show students how their lessons relate to their real lives. If students feel that lessons are relevant to them personally, they will pay more attention in class.

Review

Objective
Students will be able to consolidate their understanding of the vocabulary and grammar learned in the unit.

Lesson 11 — Student's Book p. 122

> ✔ **Homework Check!**
> Workbook p. 156, Activity 1 (Review)
>
> **Answers**
> **1 Read the messages and say how the people are feeling.**
> 1. Aaron's embarrassed. 2. Emilio's excited.
> 3. Lisa's jealous. 4. Walt's worried. 5. Atsuko's happy.

Warm-up
Students review feelings vocabulary playing a game.
- Review feelings vocabulary from pages 112 and 113 (angry, happiness, embarrassed, etc.) by playing Hangman.

1 Look at the emoticons and write the nouns. What is the mystery word?
Students identify abstract nouns for feelings using emoticons.

> **Answers**
> 1. fear, 2. embarrassment, 3. jealousy,
> 4. excitement, 5. happiness, 6. worry,
> 7. anger, 8. sadness, *Mystery word* emotions

2 Complete the chart with the words below.
Students complete a chart by categorizing feelings adjectives as positive or negative.

> **Answers**
> *Positive Adjectives* excited, happy, *Negative Adjectives* angry, embarrassed, frightened, jealous, sad, worried

3 Circle the correct options to complete the story.
Students read a story and determine whether to complete the sentences with the feelings adjective or noun.

> **Answers**
> 1. excited, 2. jealous, 3. fear, 4. worry,
> 5. embarrassment, 6. angry, 7. sad, 8. happiness

> **Extension**
> Students design their own emoticons.
> - Organize students into pairs and have them make their own new designs for emoticons to show fear, excitement, happiness, anger, etc.
> - Invite students to display their designs on a poster and to share them with the rest of the class.

Wrap-up
Students interview each other in pairs about a time when they felt a mixture of feelings.
- Invite students to ask each other about a time (true or made up) when they experienced a variety or a mixture of emotions, for example, at one moment they were worried, then they felt excitement, etc. Encourage them to use a variety of adjectives and nouns in their stories.

➡ **(No homework today.)**

Lesson 12   Student's Book p. 123

Warm-up

Students review question words.
- Write incomplete sentences such as the following on the board and have students complete them with the correct expression: *To ask about a person, we use the question word _____ . To ask about a place, we use _____ . To ask about a duration of time, we use _____ .*

Answers

who, where, how long

4 Complete the questions using the words below.

Students complete questions with the correct question words.

Answers

1. How long, 2. How much, 3. Who, 4. Why, 5. What, 6. What, 7. Where, 8. How

5 Complete the questions with auxiliary verbs. Write one word in each blank.

Students read and complete questions with the correct auxiliary verb form.

Answers

1. do, 2. will, 3. did, 4. Do, 5. is, 6. are, 7. do, 8. Can

6 Circle the correct options.

Students select the correct question word to complete the questions.

Answers

1. Which, 2. Which, 3. What, 4. What, 5. Which, 6. What, 7. Which, 8. What

? Big Question

Students are given the opportunity to revisit the Big Question and reflect on it.
- Ask students to turn to the unit opener on page 111 and to look again at the image. Discuss how the photo, which shows multiple images of the same person, was put together. Ask students to say which emotion is being shown in each of the three photos of the young man where his face can be seen clearly.
- As a whole class, talk about the way the face reveals our emotions. Talk also about other ways that we show how we are feeling (gestures, body posture, etc.).
- Discuss the fact that it is not always possible to know how a person is feeling from their outward appearance. Talk about the way some people try to hide their feelings and why they might want or need to do this.

★ Scorecard

Hand out (and/or project) a *Scorecard*. Have students fill in their *Scorecards* for this unit.

➡ **Study for the unit test.**

Verb List

Present	Past	Present	Past	Present	Past
analyze	analyzed	give	gave	record	recorded
answer	answered	go	went	remove	removed
appear	appeared	grow	grew	return	returned
arrive	arrived	hang out	hung out	ride	rode
ask	asked	happen	happened	run	ran
be	was / were	have	had	save	saved
become	became	hear	heard	say	said
begin	began	help	helped	see	saw
believe	believed	invent	invented	send	sent
break	broke	investigate	investigated	serve	served
bring	brought	join	joined	sew	sewed
buy	bought	jump	jumped	show	showed
call	called	keep	kept	sing	sang
cancel	canceled	know	knew	sit	sat
carry	carried	laugh	laughed	sleep	slept
choose	chose	learn	learned	solve	solved
come	came	like	liked	speak	spoke
consider	considered	listen	listened	spend	spent
cook	cooked	live	lived	start	started
create	created	look	looked	stay	stayed
dance	danced	lose	lost	stop	stopped
decompose	decomposed	love	loved	study	studied
describe	described	make	made	swim	swam
design	designed	meet	met	take	took
die	died	miss	missed	tell	told
discover	discovered	move	moved	think	thought
discuss	discussed	need	needed	throw	threw
do	did	notice	noticed	travel	traveled
draw	drew	open	opened	try	tried
drink	drank	paint	painted	turn	turned
eat	ate	pay	paid	use	used
encourage	encouraged	pick	picked	visit	visited
enjoy	enjoyed	plant	planted	wait	waited
exercise	exercised	play	played	walk	walked
feel	felt	practice	practiced	want	wanted
find	found	prefer	preferred	watch	watched
finish	finished	prepare	prepared	wear	wore
fly	flew	put	put	win	won
forget	forgot	rain	rained	work	worked
fry	fried	read	read	write	wrote
get	got	receive	received		